MW00513260

NS Nick Stellino
COOKING WITH FRIENDS

Nick Stellino Cooking with Friends

The companion cookbook to the popular television series

CREATIVE DIRECTION AND BOOK DESIGN
Lisa Moore

TITLE DESIGN
Rodney Shelden Fehsenfeld Jr.

PHOTOGRAPHY
Therese Frare

EDITOR
Pat Mallinson

ADDITIONAL PHOTO CREDITS
Photo of Laurent Manrique
page 138 and dust jacket
courtesy of AQUA

Photo of Neal Fraser
page 137 and dust jacket
CREDIT: Andrea Wyner

Photo of Elise Wiggins
page 139 and dust jacket
CREDIT: Larry Laszlo

ISBN 978-0-9740286-3-7

PRINTED IN KOREA

NS

Nick Stellino
COOKING WITH FRIENDS

PHOTOGRAPHS | Therese Frare

Stellino Productions
SHERMAN OAKS, CALIFORNIA

Vincenzo Stellino

1927–2007

I WOULD LIKE TO DEDICATE THIS BOOK TO MY FATHER, Vincenzo, who passed away last year. He was the man who taught me to go after my dreams, and without his teachings and guidance, I would not be the man I am today. I know he is watching me. And I'm sure that right now, he's cooking a big feast for everybody up there in the sky somewhere, all the while telling stories and talking about his two boys, Nick and Mario, as he always did.

■

table of contents

Someone's in the kitchen with Nick...

Chef Danny Bortnick 14
Firefly | Washington, DC

Chef Michael Cimarusti 20
Providence | Los Angeles

Chef Neal Fraser 32
Grace Restaurant | Los Angeles

Chef Michael Hillyer 44
The Capital Grille | Seattle

Chef Laurent Manrique 54
AQUA | San Francisco

Chef Walter Pisano 66
Tulio | Seattle

Chef Kent Rathbun 82
Abacus | Dallas ~ Jasper's Restaurants | Texas

Chef Heather Terhune 96
Atwood Café | Chicago

Chef Elise Wiggins 104
Panzano | Denver

Chef Patricia Williams 120
District | New York

table of contents

SALADS

Calamari Salad with Heirloom Tomatoes & Mint 24
Fresh Chèvre and Panzanella Salad 69
Grilled Salad with Goat Cheese 91
Hamachi with Grapefruit-Basil Salad 59
Jasper's Tomato, Grilled Asparagus and Blue Cheese Salad with Grilled Chicken 84
Palisade Peach Salad with Crispy Prosciutto-Crusted Goat Cheese Balls & Hazelnut-Mint Vinaigrette 107
Spinach Salad with Feta Cheese and Seedless Grapes 119
Tomato, Burrata and Arugula Salad 80
Watercress Salad with Poached Pears & Gorgonzola 121

SOUPS

Chestnut Soup and Nantucket Bay Scallops 57
Silky Corn Soup with Truffle Oil & King Crab Meat 76
Split Pea Chowder 123

PASTA

Bucatini with Pancetta and Ricotta 75
Herb Risotto with Heirloom Tomato Salad 68
Pasta with Cherry Tomatoes, Basil and Shrimp 50
Pasta with Ham, Mushrooms, Asparagus and Truffle Oil 18

ENTRÉES

Chicken Scaloppine with Leeks and Morels Sauce 41
Crab and Lobster Burgers 45
Day Boat Halibut with Yukon Gold Potatoes and Chive Blossoms 23
Green Eggs & Ham – Spinach, Ham and Cheese Quiche 16
Grilled Arctic Char with Chipotle Barbecue Sauce, Jicama Salad & Mango-Pineapple Salsa 99
Grilled Fillet of Beef with Farro, Haricots Verts, Italian Sausage and Red Wine Sauce 33
Grilled Skirt Steak with Tomato-Infused Marinade 79
Herb-Crusted Halibut with Fingerling Potatoes, Basil Nage, and Braised Romaine and Squash Blossoms 38
Lobster Macaroni & Cheese with Truffle Oil 83
Maryland Crab Fritters with Herb Salad and Lemon Aïoli 97
Meatballs with Tomato Sauce 15
Mushroom Crêpes with Fonduta Sauce 110
Pork Chops with Nancibella Sauce 115
Sautéed Day Boat Scallops with Truffle Risotto 36
Slow-Roasted Breast of Veal 125
Sole with Orange-Ginger Sauce 63
Striped Bass with Pistachios and Wild Mushrooms 21
Truffle-Salted Wild Salmon and Bitter Greens Salad 72
Tuna Steaks with Peperonata Sauce 128
Tuna Tartare with Grilled Toast 102
Veal Chops with Rosemary, Lemon and Honey Sauce 27
Venetian-Style Mussels 67
Wild King Salmon with Sauce Grenobloise and Cauliflower Ragoût 55
Wood-Grilled Pork Tenderloin with Peach Barbeque Sauce 86

SIDES

Bourbon Creamed Corn 87
Broiled Asparagus 30
Chipotle Barbecue Sauce 99
Corn Relish 45
Jicama Salad 99
Mango-Pineapple Salsa 99
Roasted Butternut Squash with Parmesan 31
Tartar Sauce 45

DESSERTS

Chocolate and Cherry Cake 112
Chocolate Espresso Cake with Raspberry Sauce 48
Claufouti 126
Dried Cherry-White Chocolate Bread Pudding 89
Easy Chocolate Mousse 95
Fried Palisade Peach Pie with Vanilla Gelato 105
Pears in Red Wine Sauce 132

foreword

Being on Nick's show is like getting back together with an old friend. We both love food and we both feel most at home in a kitchen, so cooking is the common language we 'speak' when we are together.

Nick reminds me to look at both my past and my future when I cook. My Italian roots, of course, helped shape my career as a chef. And my wife and children inspire me toward the future—toward what I will become in the next chapter of my life. Nick has always emphasized family as the 'spice' that completes a meal. Where I come from, it's what people remember most about their dining experiences. More so than the meal, it's the memories.

My son Giovanni is two-and-a-half. Like any typical little boy, he likes to play with toy trucks. But after watching me for so many hours, he decided he also likes to 'cook.' He has his own mini personal kitchen at our house. Though he's still very young, I think one day he will understand how the foundation of our home and our family is built on the love of food and a passion for cooking.

It is truly a treat for me to cook for Nick when he comes to Seattle. This past visit, he ate at Tulio about a half-dozen times. I know exactly what he'll order every time: the sautéed calamari. It's not on the current menu, but for Nick, anything's possible in my kitchen.

– Walter Pisano

a note from the chef...

I STARTED MY LIFE HERE IN AMERICA AS A STUDENT, then became a stockbroker, a dishwasher and a chef. Ultimately, thanks to a magical opportunity, I became a TV chef. It's been quite a beautiful adventure. As I've worked on this book, I've realized that my life has come full circle. I am no longer the young, ambitious, up-and-coming celebrity chef who launched his first public television series 14 years ago. Now, at 50 years of age, I have become an "elder" of the industry. What has transpired over the years has been phenomenal.

A year or so ago, I was at a book release party in Hollywood. It was the launch of *The Hollywood Cookbook*, in which a few of my recipes had been published, along with those of many actors and actresses, models and celebrity chefs, to raise funds for charity. There were paparazzi everywhere, snapping photos and yelling. The room was full of beautiful people, the music was loud, and the party was raging on. One of the first things I noticed upon entering the room was a thick head of red hair, accompanied by a big smile, as a man walked toward me with his hand outstretched. I recognized him right away; he was Michael Cimarusti, a culinary superstar in Los Angeles. Michael had already established a name for himself with his restaurant Providence, a real hot spot and a culinary mecca for people "in the know."

Michael reached out to shake my hand and then he started to talk, quickly and loudly, compensating for the thunderous music in the place. I took it as a real compliment that he recognized me and wanted to meet me. I couldn't hear everything he was saying, but I heard what really mattered, and it struck me like lightning. "I always wanted to meet you," he said. "When I was a little kid, I always used to watch your TV show... man, you were funny!"

My father always used to say: "Nicolino, la vita scorre come un fiume in piena" ("Nick, life runs away from you like a river rushing downhill"). I never quite understood what those words meant, until that moment. There were two ways to look at it. One way was to take partial credit for influencing the formative years of this culinary genius who was standing before me shaking my hand. The other way was to feel rather ... "mature." In a less than illustrious way, I felt the latter.

After I went home that evening, I found myself sitting in my office, reminiscing over old photos, magazine articles and souvenirs of events gone by, and as I wandered down memory lane, I said out loud, "When did time start to go by so fast?" Suddenly I understood my father's words even more clearly. So many images came rushing through my mind, such as the first time I met Jacques Pépin, one of my culinary idols. I could hardly speak the words for a proper greeting, but after working with Jacques many times over the years, I think of him as the ultimate gentleman.

As I sat in my office, I also remembered having lunch with Julia Child and famed winemaker Robert Mondavi at an event in San Francisco and recalled, too, how surreal it all was, especially when they called me by my first name. I could still feel the excitement of being Grand Marshal of the Columbus Day Italian Heritage Parade in San Francisco and of giving a speech for the first time at the James Beard Foundation

Awards. I remembered working with chef and restaurateur Mario Batali and learning firsthand from him about the Spanish chapter of his youth.

I remembered how complimented I felt when fellow public television chef Lidia Bastianich came to say hi to me when I dined at her restaurant for the first time. I had a memory of legendary restaurateur Sirio Maccioni greeting me by my first name when we ran into each other on the streets of New York; I was so excited that I called my family in Sicily to tell them what had happened. I remembered cooking for Oprah Winfrey on her show, and being in awe of the fact that I was even there.

When my father passed away last year, I became even more aware of the tenuous grasp we all have on life, and I wanted to do something completely different that would take me on a fresh adventure and in a new and different direction. I cut off my ponytail (after 14 years). I started working out vigorously with a trainer—and lost over 60 pounds! And I started formulating ideas for a new direction, including plans for my next TV series and for this cookbook.

I wanted the new project to incorporate the culinary views of some of my friends, both new and old. I wanted to play on the set of my television show, becoming a student again. I wanted to have fun, to unleash the "inner child" of other culinary professionals, and to share with my readers and viewers alike the passion that is cooking.

For the *Cooking with Friends* cookbook and television project, I had the pleasure of working with some wonderful culinary friends. Laurent Manrique from AQUA in San Francisco was the chef who introduced my nephew Andrew to his first gourmet experience; to this day, Andrew is still talking about it. Laurent was the first to accept my invitation to play in my kitchen. Kent Rathbun and I have known each other for 13 years, and he is the warmest and funniest guy you will ever meet—I just wanted to share that side of him with you. Walter Pisano and I have been "partners in crime" for a long time. His wonderful father, Tulio, first introduced us 13 years ago. The story that Walter tells about his little boy Giovanni is one of the most touching in the whole *Cooking with Friends* TV series.

Of course, I could not just stop there. I had to ask the red-haired kid who got me started with all of this, so I called Michael Cimarusti, and he also joined us. Along the way, I met a lot of other talented chefs: Patricia Williams, Elise Wiggins, Michael Hillyer, Heather Terhune, Danny Bortnick and Neal Fraser. Each and every one has a great personal story, wonderful recipes and an awesome passion for cooking. One by one, they all accepted my invitation and came on board for this project.

So here we are!

After eight cookbooks and hundreds of episodes of my TV series that have aired worldwide, I still think of myself as the boy who left Sicily 33 years ago. As I look at this book, I feel proud of the long road it took me to get here, and I must say that I have loved the journey. My professional associations, my relationships with family and friends, my successes, and even the grandest and most outlandish defeats I've suffered along the way have all combined to make me the man that I am now. When I look at where I am at this juncture of my life, I feel lucky. I have been married for over 25 years to the love of my life, Nanci, and I am proud to have met so many people along the way that I now call my friends.

Sometimes we need to stop and take a moment to acknowledge all of the wonderful things that life brings our way. We need to hold all of the things that matter most in life close to our hearts. And we need to be thankful for how lucky we are. I know that I am.

Now... start reading, then get cooking, and let us help you turn your home into your favorite restaurant!

"Cooking is about bringing people together, evoking memories, and creating new experiences.

I want my guests to take their first bite and say, 'I remember when I was a little boychick, my mom used to make this for me...
but she never made it taste this good!'"

DANNY BORTNICK

Chef Danny Bortnick

Firefly | Washington, DC

Meatballs with Tomato Sauce

Green Eggs & Ham – Spinach, Ham and Cheese Quiche

NS Pasta with Ham, Mushrooms, Asparagus and Truffle Oil

Meatballs with Tomato Sauce

DANNY BORTNICK

Makes 12 servings

2 pounds ground beef
1 pound ground pork
1 pound ground veal
5 ounces ground bacon
1 tablespoon ground fresh garlic
3 tablespoons meatball spice (See accompanying recipe.)
2 tablespoons salt
1½ cups bread crumbs
4 eggs
½ cup heavy cream

1 quart tomato sauce
12 basil leaves, for garnish
Parmesan, shaved, for garnish

FOR THE MEATBALL SPICE (yields 3 cups):
¾ cup fennel seeds
¼ cup coriander seeds
2 tablespoons cumin seeds
¼ cup black peppercorns
1 teaspoon red pepper flakes
1 tablespoon sweet paprika
1 teaspoon chili powder
2 tablespoons dried oregano
1¼ cups kosher salt
2 tablespoons C&H® or Domino® sugar

Combine all 4 ground meats with the garlic, meatball spice (preparation follows), salt, bread crumbs, eggs and heavy cream. Form into 2-ounce balls.

Sear the meatballs, browning evenly on all sides. Warm the tomato sauce with the meatballs.

TO PREPARE THE MEATBALL SPICE:
Toast the fennel, coriander, cumin and peppercorns until perfumed. Add the rest of the spices and the sugar, and grind in a coffee grinder until medium-coarse. Store in an airtight container.

TO SERVE:
Serve 4 meatballs per person, with 4 ounces of sauce over the top. Garnish with basil leaves and shaved Parmesan.

Green Eggs & Ham
Spinach, Ham and Cheese Quiche

DANNY BORTNICK

Serves 6

FOR THE PIE DOUGH:
1 pound all-purpose flour
1½ teaspoons salt
8 ounces unsalted butter, at room temperature
1 egg
1 tablespoon plus 1 teaspoon ice water
1 teaspoon lemon juice

FOR THE QUICHE FILLING (yields 6 cups):
½ bag (8 ounces) **spinach**
Ice water
1 cup smoked Virginia ham, diced
1½ cups Wisconsin Gruyère, shredded
10 eggs
2⅔ cups milk
1 cup heavy cream
1½ teaspoons salt, plus extra for blanching the spinach
1½ teaspoons black pepper
½ teaspoon nutmeg

Marinated heirloom tomatoes and purslane or watercress, for garnish

TO PREPARE THE PIE DOUGH:
Either by hand using a mixing bowl or using a stand mixer with the paddle attachment, blend together the flour, salt and butter at low speed, scraping down the sides of the bowl as necessary. Combine the egg, water and lemon juice. Incorporate the liquid with the flour mixture and blend only until it forms a dough. Do not overmix. The dough should be smooth and shiny. Cover the dough and refrigerate a minimum of 2 hours.

When the dough is well rested, roll it out to ¼-inch thickness. Place the dough over the top of a tall 9-inch springform pan and gently set it into the pan. The interior sides and bottom of the pan will need to be covered with a continuous piece of dough. The edge of the dough should slightly overhang the top of the pan (to help reduce shrinking). Place the dough back into the refrigerator and chill for 30 minutes (to help reduce cracking). Meanwhile, preheat the oven to 300 degrees. After chilling the dough, fill it with pie weights or dried beans and bake 15 to 20 minutes. Set aside to cool.

TO PREPARE THE QUICHE FILLING:
You will first need to blanch the spinach. Bring a small pot of salted water to a boil. Add the spinach. Stir for 10 to 15 seconds and drain. After it is drained, the spinach will need to be plunged into ice water to stop the cooking.

Place the ham and shredded cheese in the baked pie shell. To make the custard, combine the eggs and spinach, and purée in a blender until smooth. Add the milk and cream, and purée to combine. Season with the salt, pepper and nutmeg. Pour the custard over the ham and cheese, and bake at 325 degrees until the custard is cooked, approximately 1 hour and 40 minutes.

TO SERVE:
Let the quiche rest until it's cool enough to handle, then cut into slices and serve. Garnish each plate with marinated heirloom tomatoes and purslane or watercress.

NS Pasta with Ham, Mushrooms, Asparagus and Truffle Oil

NICK STELLINO

Serves 4 to 6

4 tablespoons Pompeian® Extra Virgin Olive Oil
4 garlic cloves, thickly sliced
1 pound asparagus, cut into ¼-inch rounds
¼ cup chopped shallots
¾ pound shiitake mushrooms, sliced
¼ pound prosciutto or ham, finely chopped (optional)
4 tablespoons chopped parsley, divided
¾ cup white wine
2 cups chicken stock or vegetable stock
1 cup cream
½ cup tomato sauce
1 pound DaVinci® Penne Rigate pasta
5 tablespoons grated Parmesan cheese
1 tablespoon Susan Rice™ Olive Oil with Summer Truffles
½ teaspoon salt or to taste
½ teaspoon pepper or to taste

In a large sauté pan, cook the olive oil and garlic over medium heat until the garlic begins to brown, about 2 minutes. Add the asparagus and cook 2 more minutes. Add the shallots, stir well, and cook 1 more minute. Add the mushrooms, the optional prosciutto and half of the parsley. Increase the heat to high and cook 1 more minute, stirring well.

Add the wine and cook 1 more minute, stirring well. Add the chicken stock, cream and tomato sauce. Bring to a boil, reduce the heat to medium-low, and cook for 15 minutes.

Cook the pasta in boiling water according to the directions on the package. Drain well and return to the pot.

Pour the sauce over the pasta and cook, stirring over medium heat, for 3 more minutes until the sauce is absorbed. Add the Parmesan cheese, truffle oil and remaining parsley. Toss well, and serve. Season with the salt and pepper.

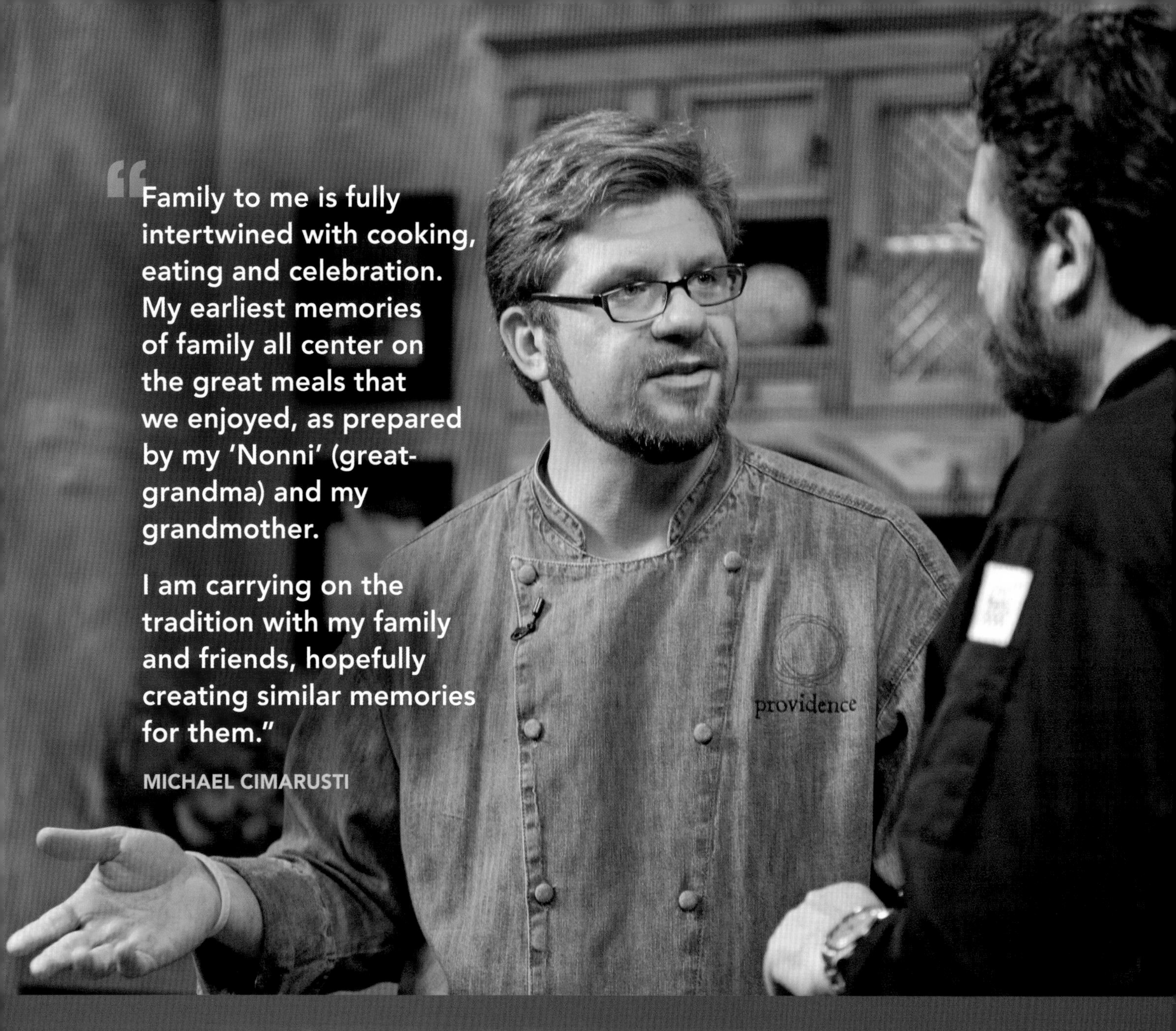

"Family to me is fully intertwined with cooking, eating and celebration. My earliest memories of family all center on the great meals that we enjoyed, as prepared by my 'Nonni' (great-grandma) and my grandmother.

I am carrying on the tradition with my family and friends, hopefully creating similar memories for them."

MICHAEL CIMARUSTI

Chef Michael Cimarusti

Providence | Los Angeles

Striped Bass with Pistachios and Wild Mushrooms

Day Boat Halibut with Yukon Gold Potatoes and Chive Blossoms

Calamari Salad with Heirloom Tomatoes & Mint

NS Veal Chops with Rosemary, Lemon and Honey Sauce

Broiled Asparagus

Roasted Butternut Squash with Parmesan

Striped Bass with Pistachios and Wild Mushrooms

MICHAEL CIMARUSTI

Serves 4

4 6-ounce fillets wild striped bass
1 to 2 tablespoons Pompeian® Extra Light Olive Oil, plus extra to grease baking sheet

FOR THE MUSHROOMS:
1 pound mixed wild mushrooms (I recommend a mix of chanterelle, shiitake and oyster.)
2 ounces whole butter
1 ounce shallots, finely chopped
1 branch thyme
Juice of ½ lemon
Salt and pepper
1 small bunch parsley, roughly chopped
½ cup shelled pistachios, salted and roughly chopped

2 ounces pure pistachio oil
1 ounce aged balsamic vinegar, the older the better, or Pompeian® Balsamic Vinegar
Toasted pistachios, for garnish

TO PREPARE THE MUSHROOMS:
Clean an assortment of your favorite mushrooms. Melt the whole butter in a small sauté pan. Add the chopped shallots and sweat them till translucent, then add the mushrooms, a branch of thyme and the juice of half a lemon. Season with salt and pepper; continue cooking the mushrooms until their juice has evaporated for the most part. At this point, remove the mushrooms from the heat and add the chopped parsley and the chopped pistachios. Keep the mushrooms warm for service.

TO PREPARE THE BASS:
Add 1 to 2 tablespoons of olive oil to a pan and cook the fillets of bass on the skin side over medium-high heat until the skin begins to crisp. When the skin becomes crispy, remove the fish from the pan and place it on a baking sheet that you have drizzled liberally with olive oil. Place the baking sheet in a preheated 250-degree oven. The time it takes for the bass to finish cooking will depend on the thickness of the fillet. Plan for about 3 minutes in the oven per inch of thickness.

TO SERVE:
Divide the mushrooms equally among 4 warmed plates. Place a fillet of bass on each plate. Drizzle the plates with a mixture of 2 parts pure pistachio oil to 1 part aged vinegar. Grate a few toasted pistachios over the plate using a Microplane or the fine side of a box grater as you would Parmesan cheese. This will carry the flavor of the pistachios throughout each bite. Serve immediately.

Day Boat Halibut
with Yukon Gold Potatoes and Chive Blossoms

MICHAEL CIMARUSTI

Serves 4

2 large Yukon Gold potatoes, peeled, diced and cooked in salted water
¼ cup softened butter
2 ounces Pompeian® Extra Virgin Olive Oil, divided
4 6-ounce portions day boat halibut (Any kind of halibut will work well.)
Salt to taste
Cayenne pepper to taste

½ cup garlic scapes, sliced finely and blanched, or freshly chopped chives
1 bunch chives with blossoms (optional)
Lemon foam (See accompanying recipe.)

FOR THE LEMON FOAM:
1 cup lemon juice
½ cup C&H® or Domino® sugar

Place the cooked potatoes in a saucepan with just enough potato broth to cover. Add the butter and 1 ounce of the olive oil to the potatoes once they begin to boil; this will form the broth that you will serve with the dish. Turn the heat to low and keep warm until ready to serve.

To begin preparing the dish, heat a nonstick skillet over a high flame. Add enough olive oil to coat the bottom of the skillet, about 1 ounce. Dry the fish with a paper towel and season both sides with salt and cayenne pepper. Reduce the heat to medium-low. Place the nicest side of each portion face down in the skillet. Cook the fish, about 2 minutes per side, then let it rest while you assemble the remainder of the dish.

TO PREPARE THE LEMON FOAM:
Mix together the lemon juice and sugar. When you are ready to serve the dish, heat the lemon mixture to just under a boil and aerate it with an immersion blender. This will create a light, lemony foam that will carry the flavor of lemon throughout the dish.

TO SERVE:
Add the garlic scapes to the potatoes and adjust the seasoning. Divide the potatoes and their broth among 4 warmed soup bowls. Place the fish on top. Garnish with the optional chive blossoms, spoon a bit of the lemon foam over, and serve immediately.

NOTE: In his restaurant, Chef Cimarusti cooks the fish on the stove on one side only, then finishes it in the oven at 200 degrees. The key is to cook the fish delicately and over very low heat.

Calamari Salad with Heirloom Tomatoes & Mint

MICHAEL CIMARUSTI

Serves 4

FOR THE CALAMARI:

1 ounce Pompeian® Extra Virgin Olive Oil
4 medium squid, cleaned and scored, tentacles cut into quarters
Salt and pepper
1 pinch chili flakes
1 branch thyme
1 clove garlic, crushed
½ cup white wine

FOR THE VINAIGRETTE DRESSING:

Juice of 2 limes
Zest of 1 lime
Salt and pepper
Pinch of C&H® or Domino® sugar
Sriracha to taste
3 ounces Pompeian® Extra Virgin Olive Oil

FOR THE HEIRLOOM TOMATOES:

1 pound assorted heirloom tomatoes of different shapes, colors and sizes
Salt (preferably Maldon Sea Salt)
Freshly milled white pepper
2 small shallots, finely chopped
1 small bunch mint

1 head yellow frisée
2 bunches arugula
2 ounces cocktail peanuts

TO PREPARE THE CALAMARI:

Heat a large skillet over high heat. Pour 1 ounce extra virgin olive oil into the pan and heat it to the smoking point. While the pan is heating, season the squid with salt and pepper and the chili flakes, and place the branch of thyme with the garlic on the squid. When the oil begins to smoke, add the seasoned squid and stir with a wooden spoon. When the squid is coated with the oil and is beginning to turn color, add the wine. The wine will create a lot of steam, and this will finish the cooking of the squid. Remove the squid to a perforated pan and place in the fridge. Collect and save any of the juices to add to the dressing.

TO PREPARE THE VINAIGRETTE DRESSING:
While the squid is cooling, prepare this simple vinaigrette using the juice of both the limes and the zest of 1 lime, salt, pepper, sugar, sriracha and 3 ounces olive oil. Add a few torn mint leaves to the dressing to add flavor.

TO PREPARE THE HEIRLOOM TOMATOES:
Core the tomatoes and cut them into smaller pieces, being sure to highlight their unique colors and shapes. Lay the tomatoes out on a parchment-covered cookie sheet in order to facilitate their seasoning. Season the tomatoes with salt and white pepper. Sprinkle the tomatoes with the chopped shallots. Chiffonade the mint and place some of it on the tomatoes as well.

Remove the squid from the fridge and add whatever juices you have collected to the vinaigrette. Drizzle the tomatoes with some of the vinaigrette.

TO SERVE:
Divide the tomatoes among 4 chilled plates. Dress the squid in a bowl with a bit of the vinaigrette and some of the mint. Place the squid on top of the tomatoes. Dress the frisée and arugula with a bit of the vinaigrette and divide the greens among the 4 plates. Shave a few of the peanuts over the salads using a Microplane; sprinkle the rest of the peanuts over the salads.

"I always wanted to grow up
to be just like my dad.
I can still see him cooking
at our big family reunions,
turning the meat over on the
BBQ and smiling, happy...
That is why I love cooking
so much. It makes me happy!"

NS Veal Chops with Rosemary, Lemon and Honey Sauce

NICK STELLINO

Serves 4

4 veal chops (totaling approximately 3 pounds), **cut approximately ¾ inch to 1 inch thick**
1 teaspoon salt
1 teaspoon pepper
3 tablespoons Pompeian® Extra Light Olive Oil
1½ tablespoons butter

FOR THE MARINADE:
Zest of 1 lemon, chopped
2 tablespoons fresh rosemary leaves
3 tablespoons Pompeian® Extra Virgin Olive Oil
2 garlic cloves, chopped
1 teaspoon salt
1 teaspoon pepper
¼ cup sherry

FOR THE ROSEMARY, LEMON AND HONEY SAUCE:
4 tablespoons Pompeian® Extra Virgin Olive Oil
8 small peeled shallots, finely chopped, or 1 medium white onion, peeled and finely chopped
4 tablespoons fresh rosemary leaves, loosely packed
2 garlic cloves, chopped
2 tablespoons honey
2 tablespoons fresh lemon juice
½ cup sherry
4 cups veal or chicken stock

TO MARINATE THE VEAL CHOPS:
Whisk all of the marinade ingredients together and pour into a resealable plastic bag containing the meat. Marinate at least 5 hours or overnight. Make the rosemary, lemon and honey sauce. (See accompanying recipe.) The sauce can be made the day before and stored in the refrigerator.

Take the meat out of the marinade; discard the marinade. Salt and pepper the meat.

TO COOK THE VEAL CHOPS:
OPTION ONE:
Brush with the extra light olive oil and grill on the barbecue on medium-high heat, about 3 to 4 minutes per side. After grilling, place the meat on a tray and cover with foil; let it rest.

OPTION TWO:
In a pan large enough to hold all the pieces of meat, preheat the extra light olive oil over high heat until it starts to sizzle. Add the meat, reduce the heat to medium, and cook for about 3 to 4 minutes per side, basting the chops with the olive oil and juices from the bottom of the pan. Place the meat on a tray and cover with foil; let it rest.

FOR BOTH OPTIONS:
In a clean sauté pan large enough to hold all the pieces of meat, bring the rosemary, lemon and honey sauce to a boil over high heat. Add the veal chops and reduce the heat to medium-low. Cook for 2 to 3 minutes, basting the meat.

Place the meat on individual plates. Increase the heat to high and cook the sauce for 1 to 2 more minutes until it thickens. Turn off the heat, add the butter, and stir well until completely melted.

TO PREPARE THE ROSEMARY, LEMON AND HONEY SAUCE:
In a saucepan, cook the olive oil over high heat for 1 minute. Add the shallots and rosemary leaves, and reduce the heat to medium. Cook for 4 minutes until the shallots have softened. Add the garlic and stir well; cook for 1 more minute. Add the honey, stir well, and cook for 1 more minute. Add the lemon juice, stir well, and cook for 2 more minutes, until the mixture has reduced by half. Increase the heat to high and add the sherry. Cook for 2 to 3 minutes, stirring well. Add the stock, bring to a boil, then reduce to a simmer. Cover the pot and let the sauce simmer for 40 minutes. Bring the sauce to a boil over medium-high heat and cook for 8 to 10 more minutes, until it thickens. Strain the sauce and discard the solids. Store the sauce in the refrigerator until ready to use it. It will keep for 2 days.

TO SERVE:
Pour some of the rosemary, lemon and honey sauce over the meat and bring the rest to the table in a sauce boat. Broiled asparagus and roasted butternut squash with Parmesan make great accompaniments for this dish. (See recipes on pages 30 and 31.)

NS Broiled Asparagus

NICK STELLINO

Serves 4 to 6

2 pounds fresh asparagus
Ice water, for cooling the asparagus
1 tablespoon Pompeian® Extra Virgin Olive Oil
2 small shallots, chopped
2 tablespoons sundried tomatoes packed in olive oil, chopped
1 tablespoon grated Parmesan cheese (optional)
Salt and pepper to taste

Peel the stalks of the asparagus using a potato peeler, then trim the bottom 2 inches of each stalk.

Cook the trimmed asparagus in a pot of boiling water for 5 minutes. Place the cooked asparagus in a bowl of ice water and let it cool for at least 5 minutes. Preheat the broiler.

In a sauté pan, cook the extra virgin olive oil over high heat for 1 minute. Add the shallots and sundried tomatoes, and reduce the heat to medium. Cook for 3 more minutes, stirring well, until the shallots are soft.

Take the asparagus stalks out of the cold water, dry them with a clean kitchen towel, and place them in an oven-safe casserole. Pour the shallot-sundried tomato mixture over them and mix well.

Place the casserole under the broiler for 2 to 3 minutes until the asparagus is warmed through and the topping has started to brown.

Place on a serving tray, sprinkle with the optional Parmesan cheese, add salt and pepper to taste, and bring to the table.

NS Roasted Butternut Squash with Parmesan

NICK STELLINO

Serves 4 to 6

1 pound peeled and cubed butternut squash, cut into dice about 1 inch thick
1 tablespoon Pompeian® Extra Light Olive Oil
Salt and pepper to taste
2 tablespoons grated Parmesan cheese

Preheat the oven to 400 degrees. Place the squash in an oven-safe pan, mix it well with the extra light olive oil, and season with the salt and pepper. Roast for 35 minutes.

Take out the cooked squash, place it in a serving bowl, and add the Parmesan cheese. Stir well and serve.

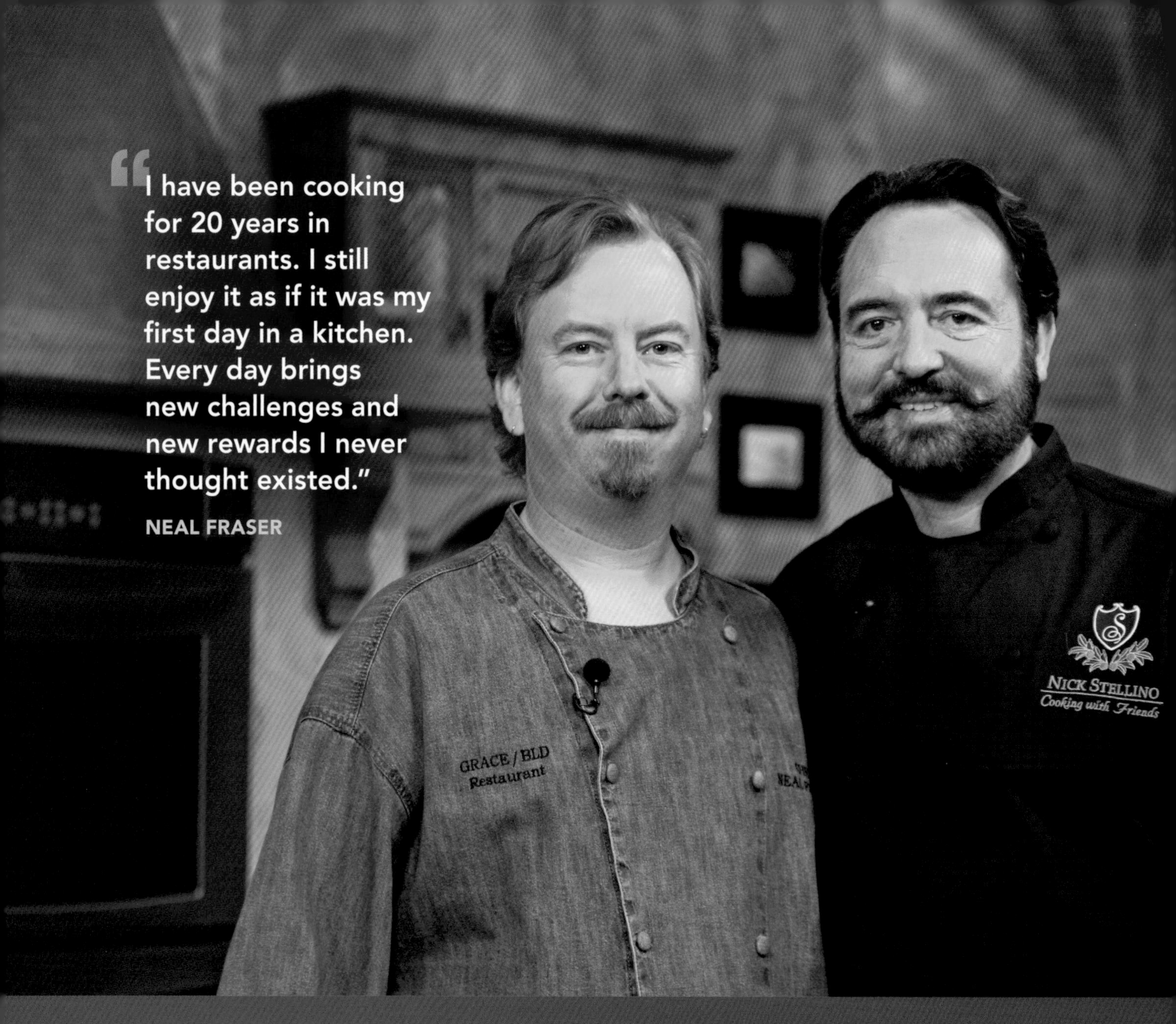

> "I have been cooking for 20 years in restaurants. I still enjoy it as if it was my first day in a kitchen. Every day brings new challenges and new rewards I never thought existed."
>
> **NEAL FRASER**

Chef Neal Fraser

Grace Restaurant | Los Angeles

Grilled Fillet of Beef with Farro, Haricots Verts, Italian Sausage and Red Wine Sauce

Sautéed Day Boat Scallops with Truffle Risotto

Herb-Crusted Halibut with Fingerling Potatoes, Basil Nage, and Braised Romaine and Squash Blossoms

NS Chicken Scaloppine with Leeks and Morels Sauce

Grilled Fillet of Beef
with Farro, Haricots Verts, Italian Sausage and Red Wine Sauce

NEAL FRASER

Serves 8

Red wine sauce (See accompanying recipe.)
Farro (See accompanying recipe.)
Haricots verts (See accompanying recipe.)
Sausage and red onions (See accompanying recipe.)
8 fillet steaks, 6 ounces each
Salt and pepper to taste
2 tablespoons Pompeian® Extra Light Olive Oil

FOR THE RED WINE SAUCE:
12 ounces red wine
12 ounces reduced veal stock or beef stock
2 ounces butter, plus 2 teaspoons softened butter if using beef stock (See Chef's Note.)
2 teaspoons flour if using beef stock (See Chef's Note.)

FOR THE FARRO:
1 onion, chopped
1 ounce Pompeian® Extra Virgin Olive Oil
2 cups farro or wheat berries, spelt berries or Kamut®
5 cups chicken stock
Salt to taste
5 ounces Parmesan cheese, grated

FOR THE HARICOTS VERTS:
1 pound haricots verts or green beans, cleaned and blanched
3 ounces butter
3 ounces chicken stock
Salt

FOR THE SAUSAGE AND RED ONIONS:
1 ounce Pompeian® Extra Virgin Olive Oil
½ pound Italian sausage, sliced
1 red onion, sliced

Prepare the red wine sauce, farro, haricots verts, and sausage and red onions, and keep warm.

Season the meat with salt and pepper to taste. Brush the fillets with extra light olive oil and grill or sauté the seasoned fillets till they reach the desired temperature.

TO PREPARE THE RED WINE SAUCE:
In a saucepan, add the wine and cook over high heat until reduced by half, about 5 to 8 minutes. Add the veal stock and bring to a boil. Reduce the heat and cook until reduced by half to a sauce-like consistency, about 15 to 20 minutes. Keep warm until ready to use. Right before serving, add the butter to the warm sauce and stir well to incorporate.

CHEF'S NOTE: If using beef stock instead of veal stock, you might need to thicken the sauce with a mixture of 2 teaspoons of softened butter and 2 teaspoons of flour. After the sauce has cooked for 15 minutes, add the butter-flour mixture a bit at a time to the sauce, until it reaches the consistency you like. You do not need to use all of the butter-flour mixture. Wait after each addition, stirring well, before you add more. The sauce will thicken up in front of your eyes.

TO PREPARE THE FARRO:
Sweat the onion in the olive oil over medium heat. Add the farro and cover with the chicken stock. Season with salt. Simmer till tender, approximately 30 to 40 minutes. Taste often as it is cooking to ensure that it has the right consistency to please your palate. Keep warm. The farro can be done a day ahead and then you can cook it to order by reheating it with a touch of chicken stock. Add the Parmesan cheese and serve.

TO PREPARE THE HARICOTS VERTS:
Heat the beans in the butter and stock, season with salt, and serve.

TO PREPARE THE SAUSAGE AND RED ONIONS:
Add the olive oil to a sauté pan and cook the sausage and onions over medium heat, stirring well, until the onions are caramelized, approximately 10 to 12 minutes.

TO SERVE:
Place the fillets on a serving plate on top of the farro, and the haricots verts on the side. Top each fillet with the sausage-and-onion mixture and dress with the red wine sauce.

Sautéed Day Boat Scallops with Truffle Risotto

NEAL FRASER

Serves 4

FOR THE TRUFFLE RISOTTO:

2 ounces butter, plus extra for seasoning
4 ounces chopped white onion
1 cup Carnaroli risotto
1 cup white wine
2 cups chicken stock, divided
Salt
2 ounces mascarpone cheese
1 ounce aged goat cheese
2 ounces Black Diamond French Truffles black or white truffles, chopped or shaved

FOR THE SAUTÉED SCALLOPS:

16 U-10 day boat scallops (U-10 is under 10 to a pound.)
Salt
Pompeian® Extra Light Olive Oil, for sautéing
1 ounce butter

TO PREPARE THE TRUFFLE RISOTTO:

In a sauce pot over medium heat, melt 2 ounces butter. Add the onion and cook until translucent.

Add the risotto and cook for 2 minutes. Add the white wine and cook until evaporated.

Add 1 cup chicken stock and cook until evaporated. Add the remaining 1 cup chicken stock and cook until evaporated.

Season with the salt, cheeses, butter, and chopped or shaved truffles. Always stir the risotto from start to finish.

TO PREPARE THE SAUTÉED SCALLOPS:

Season the scallops with salt. Heat a sauté pan on high. Add the oil and then the scallops. Add 1 ounce butter to help color the scallops. Cook till golden brown. Flip over and serve on top of a 4-ounce mound of the risotto.

Herb-Crusted Halibut
with Fingerling Potatoes, Basil Nage, and Braised Romaine and Squash Blossoms

NEAL FRASER

Serves 4

4 pieces of halibut, 5 ounces each
1 large Yukon Gold potato, cut into 4 slices
Kosher salt

FOR THE HERB CRUST:
6 ounces soft butter
8 ounces chopped herbs (basil, parsley, chives, chervil)
4 ounces brioche bread

FOR THE FINGERLING POTATOES:
8 fingerling potatoes
Salt
8 ounces Pompeian® Extra Virgin Olive Oil

FOR THE BASIL NAGE:
5 garlic cloves
4 shallots
3 ounces white wine
16 ounces chicken stock
3 ounces basil, chopped
3 ounces butter
Salt to taste

FOR THE BRAISED ROMAINE AND SQUASH BLOSSOMS:
2 heads baby romaine
10 squash blossoms
4 ounces chicken stock
Kosher salt

TO PREPARE THE HERB CRUST:
Mix the butter and herbs in a food processor till puréed. Add the bread and blend till smooth. Reserve.

TO PREPARE THE FINGERLING POTATOES:
Slice on a mandoline. Season with salt and put in a sauce pot. Cover with olive oil and simmer till fork-tender. Once cooked, drain the potatoes, then heat them in a sauté pan (to add color to the potatoes and to reheat them).

TO PREPARE THE BASIL NAGE:
Blanch the garlic and shallots by briefly plunging them into boiling water then immersing them in cold water; do this 3 times. Discard the boiling water and return the garlic and shallots to the pot; add the white wine and reduce by half. Add the chicken stock and simmer till the garlic and shallots are tender. Blend in a blender with the basil and butter till smooth. Season with salt; strain through a chinois.

TO PREPARE THE BRAISED ROMAINE AND SQUASH BLOSSOMS:
Heat in a sauté pan with chicken stock and a touch of kosher salt. Cook till tender.

TO PREPARE THE HALIBUT:
Place each piece of halibut on top of a slice of the uncooked Yukon Gold potato. Season with kosher salt, and coat the top of the fish with the herb crust mixture. Bake in a 250-degree oven till cooked through, about 10 to 14 minutes. Remove from the potato; discard the potato slices.

TO ASSEMBLE THE DISH:
Place a piece of halibut on each plate and arrange the fingerling potatoes, romaine and squash blossoms, and basil nage around it.

NS Chicken Scaloppine with Leeks and Morels Sauce

NICK STELLINO

Serves 4

2 pounds chicken scaloppine, divided
1 teaspoon salt
1 teaspoon pepper
6 to 8 tablespoons flour
8 to 10 tablespoons Pompeian® Extra Light Olive Oil, divided
4 tablespoons grated Parmesan cheese

FOR THE LEEKS AND MORELS SAUCE:
5 cups chicken stock
1 ounce dried morel mushrooms
2 tablespoons Pompeian® Extra Virgin Olive Oil
4 leeks, white part only, cut in half lengthwise, washed and then thinly sliced
1 tablespoon garlic, chopped (about 2 to 3 garlic cloves)
2½ tablespoons chopped fresh parsley, divided
½ red bell pepper, seeded and cut into small dice
½ yellow bell pepper, seeded and cut into small dice
¾ cup sherry

½ cup cream (optional)
2 tablespoons butter
Salt and pepper to taste

TO PREPARE THE LEEKS AND MORELS SAUCE:
Bring the chicken stock to a boil, turn off the heat, and add the morels. Mix well and let the dried morels steep in the hot stock for 30 minutes. Strain the morels and reserve both the stock and the morels for later use. When they're cool enough to handle, cut the morels in half lengthwise.

In a saucepan, add the olive oil and cook over high heat for 1 to 2 minutes. Reduce the heat to medium, add the leeks, and cook for 1 to 2 minutes. Add the garlic and ½ tablespoon parsley, and cook for 1 more minute, stirring well. Add the bell peppers and the reserved morels, and cook for 2 more minutes, stirring well. Increase the heat to high and add the sherry. Stir well and cook for 1 to 2 minutes until the sherry is reduced by half.

Add the strained chicken stock to the mixture and bring to a boil over high heat. Cover, then reduce the heat to medium-low and cook for 15 to 20 minutes.

Strain the sauce into another saucepan. Place the strained leeks-peppers-morels mixture in another saucepan and keep warm to serve later, with the scaloppine. For presentation purposes, pick 12 of the best-looking pieces of morels to decorate the 4 servings of scaloppine. Place the morel pieces in a small saucepan and keep warm.

Bring the strained sauce to a boil over high heat, then reduce the heat to medium. Cook for 10 to 15 minutes. The sauce can be made up to this point the day before. It will keep fresh in the refrigerator for 2 days.

When ready to serve, add the optional cream and cook over medium heat for 5 more minutes, then add the butter and stir well until all of the butter is incorporated into the sauce. Add salt and pepper to taste, sprinkle with the remaining 2 tablespoons chopped parsley, and serve.

TO PREPARE THE SCALOPPINE:
Sprinkle the scaloppine with the salt and pepper. Dust the scaloppine lightly with the flour, shaking to remove the excess. Heat half of the olive oil in a large saucepan on high, and quickly brown half of the chicken on both sides for 2 minutes. Remove from the pan and place on a paper-lined platter. Cover with foil and keep warm. Add the remaining oil to the pan and repeat with the remaining pieces of chicken.

Add the Parmesan to the leeks-peppers-morels mixture left over from the preparation of the leeks and morels sauce, and keep warm over low heat.

TO SERVE:
Place a quarter of the leeks-peppers-morels mixture in the middle of each plate. Place the chicken scaloppine around the mixture and drizzle the sauce around each serving. Decorate by placing 3 pieces of the warm morels reserved from the leeks-peppers-morels mixture on top of each serving of scaloppine.

"Sauté some fresh haricots verts
for an excellent side for the
scaloppine dish."

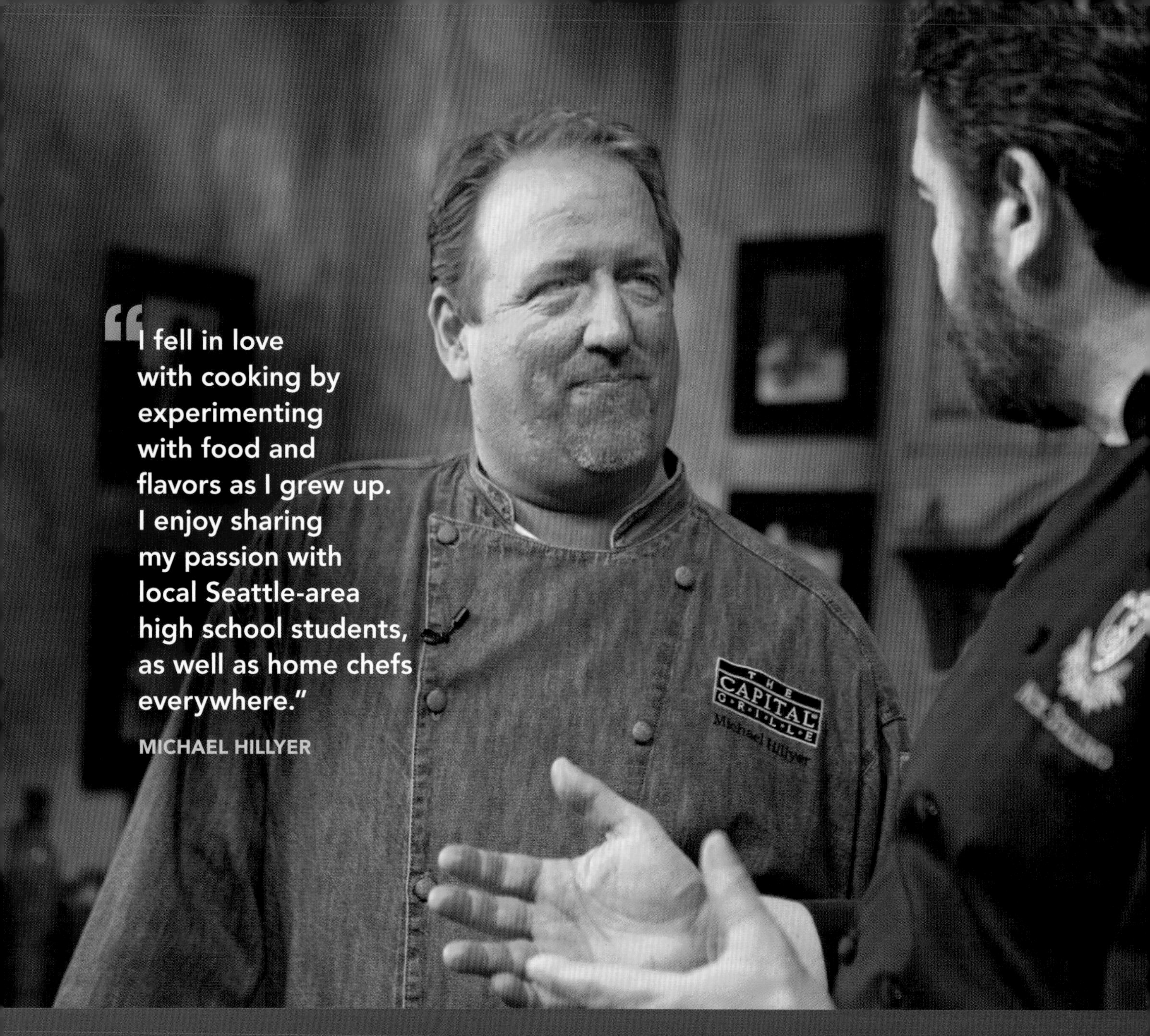

> "I fell in love with cooking by experimenting with food and flavors as I grew up. I enjoy sharing my passion with local Seattle-area high school students, as well as home chefs everywhere."
>
> MICHAEL HILLYER

Chef Michael Hillyer

The Capital Grille | Seattle

Crab and Lobster Burgers

Chocolate Espresso Cake with Raspberry Sauce

NS Pasta with Cherry Tomatoes, Basil and Shrimp

Crab and Lobster Burgers

MICHAEL HILLYER

Serves 4

1 pound lobster meat, broken into pieces (largest piece ¾ inch)
1 pound Dungeness crabmeat
1 teaspoon dry mustard
1 teaspoon Worcestershire sauce
1 teaspoon parsley, freshly chopped
2 eggs, beaten
¾ cup mayonnaise
¼ teaspoon onion powder
¼ teaspoon kosher salt
½ cup plain bread crumbs
2 tablespoons unsalted butter, preferably clarified
4 brioche buns or hamburger buns

FOR THE TARTAR SAUCE (yields 1½ cups):
1 cup mayonnaise
¼ cup half-sour pickles, seeds removed, diced
1 tablespoon red onion, diced
1 tablespoon celery (with leaves), **diced**
1 tablespoon parsley, freshly chopped
1½ tablespoons fresh lemon juice
1 tablespoon capers
2 teaspoons caper juice (from the jar)
⅛ teaspoon kosher salt
Pinch ground white pepper
Pinch cayenne pepper

FOR THE CORN RELISH (yields 2 cups):
3 ears corn (¾ pound of corn), **freshly shucked**
Ice water, for shocking the corn
⅓ cup red bell peppers, diced
⅓ cup red onion, diced
2 tablespoons parsley, chopped
2 tablespoons Pompeian® Extra Virgin Olive Oil
½ tablespoon Pompeian® Red Wine Vinegar
¼ teaspoon kosher salt
Black pepper, freshly ground, to taste

Preheat the oven to 350 degrees. *Gently* squeeze all of the excess moisture from the lobster and crab meats. Carefully examine the lobster and crab meat a handful at a time and remove any shell fragments. Set aside. Mix the dry mustard, Worcestershire, parsley, eggs, mayonnaise, onion powder and salt in a large mixing bowl, then fold in the cleaned lobster and crab meat. Stir until just combined to maintain the texture of the seafood. Gently fold in the bread crumbs and mix until just combined. *Do not add more bread crumbs.*

Allow the mixture to rest so the bread crumbs have adequate time to absorb any excess moisture. The crab cakes should be extremely moist and tender, just to the point of falling apart. Divide the crab cake mixture into 4 portions and shape into burger forms that fit the buns. Heat the clarified butter in a skillet until just smoking and sauté the crab burgers over medium heat until golden brown. Move them to a baking tray and place in the oven for 2 to 3 minutes to ensure the centers are hot.

While the crab burgers are roasting, toast the brioche buns. Serve the burgers in the buns with a dollop of tartar sauce and a side of corn relish. (See accompanying recipes.)

TO PREPARE THE TARTAR SAUCE:
Combine all of the ingredients in a stainless steel or glass mixing bowl and mix thoroughly until combined. Place ½ cup of the tartar sauce in a food processor and pulse until all ingredients are blended. Combine the puréed mixture into the original bowl and stir well. Keep refrigerated until ready to serve. This sauce is best made the night before to allow the flavors to develop.

TO PREPARE THE CORN RELISH:
Place the peeled ears of corn, with all silk removed from the exterior of each cob, in boiling water. Simmer for 7 minutes, drain, and shock in ice water. Holding the cob by the root end, slide a paring knife toward the cutting board, cutting the corn kernels from the cob. Place the corn in a stainless steel or glass mixing bowl. Add all of the other ingredients and mix well. Refrigerate until you are ready to use.

Chocolate Espresso Cake with Raspberry Sauce

MICHAEL HILLYER

Yields 1 cake

FOR THE CAKE:

1 pound E. Guittard Semisweet Chocolate, coarsely chopped
1 pound unsalted butter, diced
1 cup freshly brewed espresso
1 cup C&H® Golden Brown or Domino® Light Brown sugar
8 eggs
Hot water, for a bath for the cake pan

Cocoa powder, for dusting the finished cake
Fresh raspberries, for garnish
Raspberry sauce, for garnish (See accompanying recipe.)

FOR THE RASPBERRY SAUCE:

1½ pounds raspberries
¼ pound C&H® or Domino® sugar
½ teaspoon salt

TO PREPARE THE CAKE (1 day before serving)**:**

Preheat the oven to 350 degrees. Line the bottom of a 9-inch-diameter cake pan with 2-inch-high sides with parchment. Place all of the chocolate in a large bowl. Bring the butter, espresso and sugar to a boil in a medium saucepan, stirring to dissolve the sugar. Add the chocolate; whisk until smooth, and let cool slightly. Whip the eggs till blended. Stir the eggs into the chocolate mixture till they are blended into it. (Do not whip.) Pour the batter into the prepared pan. Place the cake pan in a roasting pan. Pour enough hot water into the roasting pan to come halfway up the sides of the cake pan. Bake until the center of the cake is set and a tester inserted into the center comes out with a few moist crumbs attached, about 45 minutes.

Remove the pan from the water and chill the cake overnight. Cut around the pan sides to loosen the cake. Using oven mitts, hold the pan bottom over a burner set on low heat for 15 seconds, warming slightly to release the cake. (Or you can loosen the cake by placing the pan in a warm-water bath or heating the outside of the pan with a cooking torch.) Place a platter over the pan. Hold the pan and platter together tightly, and invert. Lift off the cake pan, peel off the parchment, and dust the top of the cake with cocoa powder. Cut the cake into 10 slices and garnish with fresh raspberries and raspberry sauce.

TO PREPARE THE RASPBERRY SAUCE (1 day before serving)**:**

In a medium mixing bowl, combine the raspberries, sugar and salt. Cover and refrigerate overnight. Combine all ingredients in a blender, purée, and strain through a chinois.

NS Pasta with Cherry Tomatoes, Basil and Shrimp

NICK STELLINO

Serves 4 to 6

1 teaspoon salt
½ teaspoon pepper
½ teaspoon onion powder
½ teaspoon garlic powder
½ teaspoon paprika
2 pounds shrimp, shelled and deveined
6 tablespoons Pompeian® Extra Virgin Olive Oil
1 onion, finely chopped
6 garlic cloves, thinly sliced
2 pounds cherry tomatoes, cut in half, or heirloom tomatoes, cut in quarters
¼ teaspoon C&H® or Domino® sugar (optional)
4 tablespoons chopped basil, divided
1 pound DaVinci® pasta—penne rigate or spaghetti
Salt and pepper to taste

Bring a pot of water to a boil for the pasta.

Mix the salt, pepper, onion powder, garlic powder and paprika together. Sprinkle the spice mixture over both sides of the shrimp and set aside. In a large sauté pan, cook the oil over high heat until it starts to sizzle, about 1 to 2 minutes. Add the shrimp and cook for 2 minutes. Using a slotted spoon, lift the shrimp out of the pan and place on a tray lined with paper towels to absorb the excess oil. Reduce the heat to medium and add the onion and garlic to the pan, stirring well. Cook for 2 to 3 minutes until the onion starts to soften. Add the tomatoes; add the optional sugar if they are not sweet enough. Cook, stirring, for 3 minutes. Add half of the basil and increase the heat to high. Stir well and bring to a boil. Cook for 1 minute, continuing to stir well, then cover the pan and reduce the heat to simmer, cooking for 10 more minutes.

While the sauce is simmering, add the pasta to the boiling water and cook according to the directions on the package. While the pasta is cooking, add the shrimp to the sauce. Stir well, cover again, and continue to cook on simmer for 3 to 4 minutes. Drain the pasta and return it to the pot. Pour the sauce over the pasta and cook it over medium heat, stirring, for 2 to 3 minutes. Add the remaining basil, toss well, and serve. Season with salt and pepper to taste.

CHEF'S TIP: If you want a different look, cut the shrimp into ¼-inch dice before you add it to the tomato sauce.

If the sauce is reducing too much and becoming dry, add ¼ cup of the pasta water.

"While many other Italians do not like Parmesan cheese on their seafood pasta, I love it, so I add plenty of grated Parmesan to this pasta."

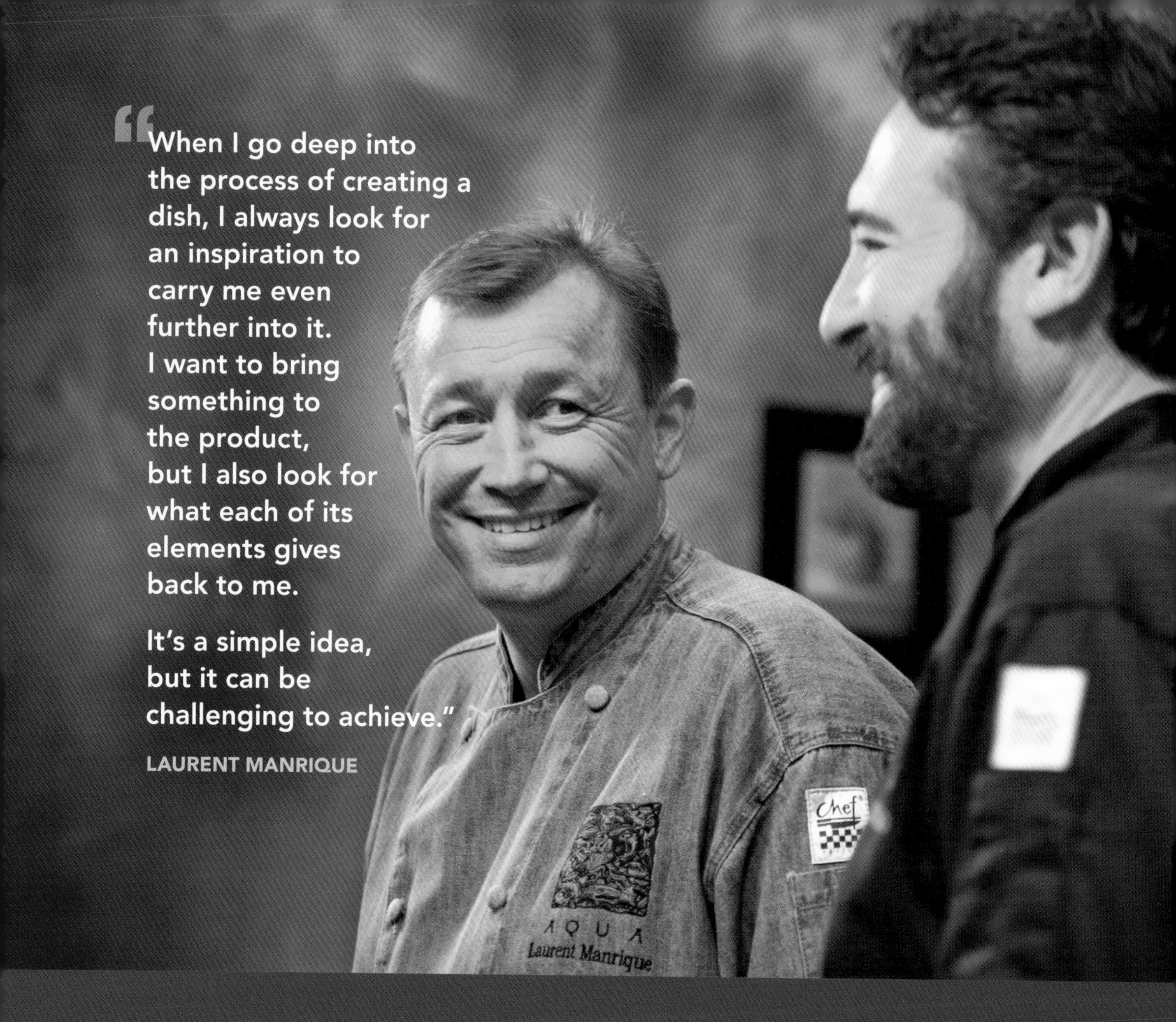

"When I go deep into the process of creating a dish, I always look for an inspiration to carry me even further into it. I want to bring something to the product, but I also look for what each of its elements gives back to me.

It's a simple idea, but it can be challenging to achieve."

LAURENT MANRIQUE

Chef Laurent Manrique

AQUA | San Francisco

Wild King Salmon with Sauce Grenobloise and Cauliflower Ragoût

Chestnut Soup and Nantucket Bay Scallops

Hamachi with Grapefruit-Basil Salad

NS Sole with Orange-Ginger Sauce

Wild King Salmon
with Sauce Grenobloise and Cauliflower Ragoût

LAURENT MANRIQUE

Serves 4

1½ pounds skinless wild king salmon fillet, cut into 8 equal pieces
Salt and pepper
2 tablespoons Pompeian® Extra Virgin Olive Oil

FOR THE CAULIFLOWER RAGOÛT:
½ cup unsalted butter
¼ cup Pompeian® Extra Virgin Olive Oil
1 head cauliflower, cut into very small florets
Kosher salt and fresh-ground black pepper to taste
½ tablespoon fresh thyme leaves
¼ cup champagne vinegar or Pompeian® Pomegranate Infused Balsamic Vinegar
¼ cup dry white wine
½ cup chicken stock
¼ cup golden raisins
1 tablespoon minced shallots
½ cup heavy cream

FOR THE SAUCE GRENOBLOISE:
½ cup unsalted butter
2½ cups diced sourdough bread, crusts removed
4 tablespoons capers, rinsed
4 tablespoons diced lemon segments
1 tablespoon sherry vinegar
1 cup fresh Italian parsley, cut into thin strips
Salt and pepper to taste

TO PREPARE THE CAULIFLOWER RAGOÛT:
In a large sauté pan over medium-high heat, cook ½ cup butter and ¼ cup oil. Add the cauliflower, season with salt and pepper, and cook for 6 minutes, carefully turning the florets with a spatula. Sprinkle in the thyme and cook until the cauliflower is golden brown, another 6 to 8 minutes.

Add the champagne vinegar and wine to the pan and reduce until the pan is almost dry, 5 to 10 minutes. Add the chicken stock, raisins and shallots, and cook 3 minutes.

Add the heavy cream and boil the sauce over medium-high heat until it is thick enough to coat the back of a spoon, 3 to 5 minutes. Remove the cauliflower ragoût from the heat and set aside.

TO PREPARE THE SAUCE GRENOBLOISE:
In a medium sauté pan over high heat, melt ½ cup butter and cook to golden brown, about 2 minutes. Add the bread and sauté until golden, 8 to 10 minutes. Add the capers and lemon segments, and immediately remove from the heat. Add the sherry vinegar and the parsley, and salt and pepper to taste. Set the Sauce Grenobloise aside.

TO PREPARE THE SALMON:
Season both sides of the salmon with salt and pepper. Warm 2 tablespoons oil in a nonstick sauté pan over low heat. Add the salmon and cook 2 to 3 minutes. Turn the fish carefully, and continue to cook until medium-rare, 1 to 3 minutes more.

TO SERVE:
Place 2 pieces of salmon on each plate, putting the cauliflower ragoût between the pieces. Spoon the Sauce Grenobloise over the fish and serve immediately.

Chestnut Soup and Nantucket Bay Scallops

LAURENT MANRIQUE

Serves 4

FOR THE SOUP:

3 tablespoons unsalted butter, divided
1 pound fresh (or frozen and thawed) **chestnuts, peeled and chopped**
(Avoid using jarred chestnuts, which are too sweet.)
1 cup diced yellow onion
1 teaspoon kosher salt, plus more to taste
½ teaspoon fresh-ground black pepper, plus more to taste
1½ cups sherry
1 tablespoon minced garlic
8 cups duck stock (or 4 cups chicken stock and 4 cups veal stock)
6 sprigs fresh thyme, wrapped in kitchen twine

FOR THE SCALLOPS:

2 tablespoons unsalted butter, divided
2 ribs celery, diced
12 Nantucket bay scallops (or 4 large sea scallops)
2 teaspoons crème fraîche
1 tablespoon minced chives

TO PREPARE THE CHESTNUT SOUP:

In a large pot over medium heat, cook 2 tablespoons butter just until browned, 2 minutes. Add the chestnuts and sauté until crisp and golden brown, 5 minutes. Add the onion, 1 teaspoon salt and ½ teaspoon pepper, and cook until golden brown, 5 minutes. Add the sherry and garlic, and stir to deglaze the pot. Increase the heat and reduce the mixture by half. Add the stock and thyme sprigs, reduce the heat, and simmer for 20 minutes. Remove the pot from the heat and discard the thyme. Purée the soup and set aside.

TO PREPARE THE SCALLOPS:

Melt 1 tablespoon butter in a small pan over medium heat. Add the celery and sauté until just tender, 2 to 3 minutes. Keep warm. In a large sauté pan over high heat, melt 1 tablespoon butter until slightly brown. Add the scallops in a single layer and cook until light golden brown, about 30 seconds per side. Remove the pan from the heat, and add the warm celery.

TO COMPLETE:

Bring the chestnut soup to a simmer over low heat, then whisk in 1 tablespoon of butter. Evenly divide the scallops and celery among 4 bowls. Spoon ½ teaspoon of crème fraîche into each bowl, and follow with ¼ tablespoon of chives and a pinch of pepper. Pour the warm soup around the scallops and serve immediately.

Hamachi with Grapefruit-Basil Salad

LAURENT MANRIQUE

Serves 4

1/4 cup fresh basil, chopped
1/4 cup plus 1/2 tablespoon canola oil or Pompeian® Extra Light Olive Oil
4 hamachi (white) **skinless fillets, 3/4 pound each**
Kosher salt and fresh-ground black pepper to taste
1 ripe avocado
Juice of 1 lime
1 grapefruit, rind removed, flesh segmented and finely diced
1/2 cup pine nuts, toasted
1 tablespoon fleur de sel or other fine sea salt
Several pinches piment d'Espelette (a ground Basque chili pepper) **or hot paprika or chili powder**
2 tablespoons micro celery (or minced celery)

In a small bowl, combine the basil with 1/4 cup canola oil. Use a fork or small whisk to blend the mixture until some, but not all, of the basil is puréed. Set the basil oil aside to rest.

Generously season the hamachi with salt and pepper. In a nonstick pan over high heat, sear the hamachi in 1/2 tablespoon of canola oil until golden brown, 12 to 15 seconds per side. The inside will be rare. Immediately remove the fillets from the pan. Just before serving, cut each fillet into 4 equal pieces, slicing against the grain.

Cut the avocado (with rind intact) into quarters, discarding the pit. Slice each quarter diagonally into thin strips. Taking care not to mash them, separate the avocado strips from the rind, and fan out the slices in a single layer on a plate. Sprinkle with lime juice, and set aside.

In a medium bowl, combine the grapefruit, basil oil and pine nuts. Gently mix, and season with salt and pepper to taste. Set the grapefruit-basil salad aside.

TO SERVE:
Arrange 4 hamachi slices flat on the right side of a plate. Line up a quarter of the avocado slices to the left of the fish. Sprinkle 1/4 tablespoon fleur de sel and a pinch of piment d'Espelette over the avocado, and garnish the fish with 1/2 tablespoon of micro celery. Spoon a quarter of the grapefruit-basil salad on top of the hamachi. Repeat with the remaining plates, and serve.

"His hands moved quickly and elegantly; the knife blade sliced across the avocado with stealthlike precision. A quick push against the hand, and voila! All the little slices of avocado stood up in a perfect line!"

NS Sole with Orange-Ginger Sauce

NICK STELLINO

Serves 4

1½ to 1¾ pounds sole (Dover or Petrale), **skinned and boned**
6 tablespoons Pompeian® Extra Light Olive Oil
1 tablespoon chopped parsley

FOR THE BATTER:
½ cup flour
¼ cup cream
2 eggs
1 tablespoon cornstarch (optional)
½ teaspoon salt

FOR THE ORANGE-GINGER SAUCE:
2 tablespoons Pompeian® Extra Virgin Olive Oil
½ white onion, chopped
1 tablespoon ginger, peeled and chopped
1 tablespoon orange zest, chopped
1 tablespoon garlic (about 2 to 3 garlic cloves), **chopped**
¼ pound fillet of sole, chopped (optional)
½ cup sherry
1 cup orange juice
2 cups chicken stock (or, for a more complex flavor, 1 cup fish stock and 1 cup chicken stock)
1 orange, peeled and sectioned (optional)
2 tablespoons butter
2 tablespoons parsley, chopped

Make the orange-ginger sauce (see accompanying recipe) and keep warm.

TO PREPARE THE FILLETS:
Using a blender, mix the flour, cream and eggs—adding the optional cornstarch for a fluffier coating—and salt. Place the fish fillets in a large baking dish and pour the egg-and-flour mixture over the fish. Turn each fillet to make sure that it is well coated with the egg-and-flour batter, handling gently so as not to break the delicate fillets.

In a large sauté pan, cook the extra light olive oil over high heat until it starts to sizzle, about 2 to 3 minutes. One at a time, lift the fish fillets from the egg-and-flour batter and place in the hot oil. (You might need to do this in 2 batches.) Cook the fish, 1 to 2 minutes per side, until it starts to brown. Lift the fish from the pan with a fish spatula and place on a tray lined with a paper towel. Pat the top of each fillet with another paper towel to absorb the extra oil.

TO PREPARE THE ORANGE-GINGER SAUCE:
Cook the extra virgin olive oil in a saucepan over high heat for 1 to 2 minutes. Reduce the heat to medium, add the onion and ginger, and cook for 1 to 2 minutes. Add the orange zest and garlic. Cook 1 more minute, stirring well; add the optional chopped sole, and cook 1 more minute. Increase the heat to high and add the sherry. Stir well and cook for 1 to 2 minutes until reduced by half. Add the orange juice and stock (or stocks). Bring to a boil over high heat, cover, then reduce the heat to medium-low and cook for 25 minutes.

Strain the sauce into another saucepan and dispose of the strained solids. Bring the liquid to a boil over high heat, then reduce the heat to medium and cook for 10 to 15 minutes until it thickens to a sauce-like consistency and coats the back of a spoon. The sauce can be made up to this point the day before. It will keep fresh in the refrigerator for 2 days.

Just before serving, add the optional sections of peeled orange and the butter to the orange-ginger sauce. Cook over low heat for 1 to 2 minutes and stir gently until the butter has completely melted into the sauce and the orange sections have warmed through.

TO SERVE:
Place a sole fillet in the middle of each dish and top with the orange-ginger sauce. Sprinkle the chopped parsley over the sauce, and serve.

"My father used to say, 'Always look at the eyes first.' To this day when I shop for fresh fish, the eyes are the first thing I look at to gauge its freshness. And remember, if the fish has a strong fishy smell, then it isn't fresh."

"Nick has always emphasized family as the 'spice' that completes a meal. Where I come from, it's what people remember most about their dining experiences.

More so than the meal, it's the memories."

WALTER PISANO

Chef Walter Pisano

Tulio | Seattle

Venetian-Style Mussels
Herb Risotto with Heirloom Tomato Salad
Fresh Chèvre and Panzanella Salad
Truffle-Salted Wild Salmon and Bitter Greens Salad
Bucatini with Pancetta and Ricotta

NS

Silky Corn Soup with Truffle Oil & King Crab Meat
Grilled Skirt Steak with Tomato-Infused Marinade
Tomato, Burrata and Arugula Salad

Venetian-Style Mussels

WALTER PISANO

Serves 8 to 10

3 pounds mussels, cleaned
2 tablespoons Pompeian® Extra Virgin Olive Oil
1 garlic clove, sliced in half
¼ teaspoon chili flakes
5 ripe tomatoes, peeled and seeded, cut into small dice
Zest of 1 lemon
¼ cup brandy
½ cup fresh basil, sliced
3 tablespoons fresh Italian parsley, sliced

Scrub the outside shells of the mussels well, run under cold water, and remove the "beard" (the growth attached to the shell). Place in the refrigerator to keep cold.

Heat the olive oil in a large saucepan, add the garlic clove, and cook over medium heat until the garlic turns golden brown; then add the chili flakes. Next, add the mussels, stirring constantly for 1 to 2 minutes, and then cover the pan. Frequently check the mussels by removing the pan cover. They will begin to open in about 4 to 5 minutes. Once the mussels open, add the tomatoes, lemon zest and brandy. Cover the pan and cook for another 2 minutes. Remove the cover and add the basil and parsley. Lightly toss for 30 seconds.

For presentation, remove half of each mussel shell. Place the mussels-on-the-half-shell on a platter and spoon the sauce over the top. Serve immediately.

Herb Risotto with Heirloom Tomato Salad

WALTER PISANO

Serves 4

FOR THE HERB RISOTTO:

4 tablespoons unsalted butter, plus extra butter, softened, to finish
2 tablespoons Pompeian® Extra Virgin Olive Oil
1 white onion, finely diced
1 leek, washed and finely diced
1½ cups Arborio rice
1 gallon vegetable broth, strained and warmed
Fresh herbs (chives, marjoram, basil, thyme, chervil), **washed and lightly chopped—not finely minced**
Salt and white pepper to taste

FOR THE HEIRLOOM TOMATO SALAD:

8 baby heirlooms, washed and cut in half
1 whole heirloom, washed and cut into 1-inch pieces
Parmigiano-Reggiano, shaved
Sea salt and fresh black pepper
4 tablespoons Pompeian® Extra Virgin Olive Oil

TO PREPARE THE HERB RISOTTO:

In a heavy-bottomed sauce pot, start heating 4 tablespoons butter and 2 tablespoons extra virgin olive oil, and add the diced white onion and leeks. Cook on medium heat, stirring constantly, until they are soft. Add the rice and start toasting it. When this is done, begin to add the warm strained vegetable broth, adding a ladle at a time and stirring with a wooden spoon. Continue to slowly add the broth. When the risotto is almost done, add the fresh herbs and mix well. This process should use approximately 4 cups of broth. To test the risotto for doneness, take a little rice grain out and taste it—the rice should have a little crunch. If the risotto is too crunchy, continue to add broth, but very small amounts at a time. When the risotto is done, finish with softened butter and season with salt and white pepper. Then place into serving bowls.

TO PREPARE THE HEIRLOOM TOMATO SALAD:

Place the tomatoes, shaved Parmesan, salt and black pepper in a small mixing bowl. Lightly dress with 4 tablespoons extra virgin olive oil. Finish with more shaved Parmesan, gently toss all of the ingredients, and use to garnish the top of each serving of risotto. Serve immediately.

Fresh Chèvre and Panzanella Salad

WALTER PISANO

Serves 8

2½ pounds fresh baby tomatoes, such as grape tomatoes
½ red onion, cut into small dice
1 dozen fresh basil leaves, washed and sliced
1 teaspoon fresh rosemary, washed and chopped
½ teaspoon fresh sage, washed and sliced
1 tablespoon fresh chives, washed and cut into small dice
3 cups focaccia (day-old works best), **cut into ¼-inch squares**
¼ cup Pompeian® Extra Virgin Olive Oil, plus extra for drizzling on salad if desired
Sea salt and fresh black pepper to taste
1½ pounds fresh Port Madison Farm chèvre (or your favorite chèvre)

Toss the above ingredients (except the chèvre) lightly in a mixing bowl and season with salt and fresh pepper. Place in individual bowls and garnish with the chèvre. Drizzle with additional olive oil if needed.

Truffle-Salted Wild Salmon and Bitter Greens Salad

WALTER PISANO

Serves 4

4 fresh 6-ounce salmon fillets
1 tablespoon Susan Rice™ Truffle Salt
1 tablespoon Pompeian® Extra Virgin Olive Oil

FOR THE SALAD:
1 head escarole, washed and sliced into ½-inch pieces
1 head Belgian endive, washed and sliced into ½-inch pieces
1 head radicchio di Treviso, washed and sliced into ½-inch pieces
1 head radicchio, washed and sliced into ½-inch pieces
1 head frisée, washed and sliced into ½-inch pieces
3 tablespoons chives, washed and sliced into ½-inch pieces

FOR THE SALAD DRESSING:
1 tablespoon fresh lemon juice
1½ tablespoons white balsamic vinegar or Pompeian® Pomegranate Infused Blush Balsamic Vinegar
4 tablespoons Pompeian® Extra Virgin Olive Oil
1 tablespoon Susan Rice™ Olive Oil with Summer Truffles
Sea salt and fresh white pepper to taste

TO PREPARE THE SALMON:
Pre-salt the salmon with the truffle salt and let sit for 10 minutes.

In a medium-bottomed sauté pan, heat 1 tablespoon olive oil over high heat. Add the truffle-salted salmon to the pan, then turn the heat to medium-low, making sure the fish cooks slowly. This process should take about 6 to 8 minutes, depending on the thickness of the salmon fillet. Don't turn the salmon over in the pan unless you prefer medium to medium-well.

Wash all of the bitter greens and strain well. Set aside in the refrigerator.

TO PREPARE THE SALAD:
Make sure all of the greens are completely dry. In a large mixing bowl, use equal parts of each green and gently toss with the chives and dressing, reserving some of the dressing to drizzle on the fish.

TO PREPARE THE SALAD DRESSING:
In a small mixing bowl, blend together the lemon juice, the white balsamic vinegar, 4 tablespoons olive oil, the truffle oil, and the salt and pepper. Set aside.

To finish, place the greens on individual plates. Place the salmon on the greens and drizzle a small amount of dressing on the fish. Serve immediately.

Bucatini with Pancetta and Ricotta

WALTER PISANO

Serves 4 to 6

FOR THE SAUCE:

¼ cup unsalted butter
3 tablespoons Pompeian® Extra Virgin Olive Oil
1 cup pancetta, cut into ¼-inch dice
2 leeks, white part only, washed and cut into ¼-inch dice
3 tablespoons white balsamic vinegar or Pompeian® Pomegranate Infused Blush Balsamic Vinegar
⅛ teaspoon fresh rosemary, minced
3 cups chicken stock
Fresh-ground black pepper and kosher salt to taste

FOR THE PASTA:

1 pound DaVinci® pasta – bucatini or spaghetti
½ cup Italian parsley, washed and sliced

1 cup fresh ricotta, for garnish

TO PREPARE THE SAUCE:

In a heavy-bottomed saucepan, slowly heat the butter and olive oil. Add the diced pancetta and sauté until slightly crispy. This should take about 10 minutes; make sure the heat is not too high. Then add the diced leeks and sauté until soft. Deglaze with the white balsamic vinegar and reduce the liquid by half. Add the fresh rosemary and chicken stock, and again reduce the liquid by half. Turn the sauce off and season with the ground pepper and salt to taste.

TO PREPARE THE PASTA:

In a heavy-bottomed sauce pot, boil 2 gallons of salted water. When the water is boiling, submerge the pasta in the pot. (Make sure the water covers the pasta completely.) Cook the pasta according to the directions on the package. Drain the pasta well and place back into the pot. Pour the sauce on top and cook for a minute over low heat. Toss the parsley with the pasta to finish.

TO SERVE:

Place the pasta in individual bowls. Garnish by sprinkling fresh ricotta on top. Serve immediately.

CHEF'S NOTE: For optimum results, cook the pasta al dente, which is usually about 1 or 2 minutes less than called for in the package directions. That is how Italians usually do it at home!

NS Silky Corn Soup with Truffle Oil & King Crab Meat

NICK STELLINO

Serves 4

FOR THE SOUP:
4 tablespoons Pompeian® Extra Virgin Olive Oil
3 small shallots, finely chopped
1 pound whole-kernel corn
¼ cup sherry
4 cups chicken stock
¼ cup cream
1 tablespoon C&H® or Domino® sugar
Salt and pepper to taste

FOR THE CRAB MIXTURE:
3 tablespoons butter
2 tablespoons red bell pepper, finely diced
1 tablespoon chopped chives
½ pound king crab meat, cut into ¼-inch pieces, or lump crabmeat
2 tablespoons brandy

1 tablespoon Susan Rice™ Black Winter Truffle Olive Oil

TO PREPARE THE SOUP:
In a sauté pan, cook the oil over medium heat until it is hot, about 1 minute. Add the shallots and cook, stirring well, for 3 minutes. Add the corn kernels and continue to cook for 3 more minutes, stirring well. Increase the heat to high, add the sherry, and cook for 2 more minutes, stirring well. Add the stock and bring the soup to a boil. Cover the pan, reduce the heat to simmer, and cook for 30 minutes. Let the soup cool, then place in a food processor and process for 2 minutes. Strain the soup into a clean saucepan, add the cream and sugar, and bring to a boil over high heat. Reduce the heat to simmer and cook uncovered for 20 minutes, stirring every 5 minutes. Adjust salt and pepper to taste.

While the soup is cooking, prepare the crab mixture.

TO PREPARE THE CRAB MIXTURE:
In a sauté pan, cook the butter over medium-high heat for 1 minute until it is hot. Add the red bell pepper and chives; cook, stirring well, for 1 more minute. Add the crabmeat, increase the heat to high, and cook for 1 more minute. Add the brandy (being careful, as it might flame) and stir well. Cook for 1 more minute, then turn off the heat. Cover and keep warm.

TO SERVE:
Pour the soup into 4 bowls and drizzle with the truffle oil. Top each bowl of soup with a quarter of the crab mixture, and serve.

CHEF'S TIP: For a smoother soup, strain it a second time before serving it.

"Skirt steak is one of those undervalued cuts of meat that has great flavor and can easily be enhanced with a myriad of marinades to improve its natural taste."

NS

Grilled Skirt Steak with Tomato-Infused Marinade

NICK STELLINO

Serves 4 to 6

2½ to 3 pounds skirt steak

FOR THE MARINADE:

5 garlic cloves
½ cup fresh mint, loosely packed
1 tablespoon fresh thyme leaves
1 cup fresh parsley, loosely packed
1 cup fresh basil, loosely packed
1½ tablespoons salt
1 tablespoon fresh rosemary
1 28-ounce can Italian-style peeled tomatoes
½ cup Pompeian® Extra Virgin Olive Oil
½ cup Pompeian® Pomegranate Infused Balsamic Vinegar
2 tablespoons C&H® or Domino® sugar

TO MARINATE THE MEAT:

Place all of the ingredients for the marinade in a food processor and process for 2 minutes into a smooth liquid paste. Place the meat in a large resealable plastic bag and cover with the marinade. Seal the bag and swish the marinade around to make sure it coats all of the meat. Let the meat marinate in the refrigerator for at least 5 hours—preferably overnight—turning twice.

TO COOK THE MEAT:

Preheat the grill or the broiler to high.

Cook the skirt steak 4 to 6 minutes per side, according to your liking. Cover it with foil and let it rest for a few minutes.

TO SERVE:

Cut the skirt steak into slices and serve with tomato, burrata and arugula salad. (See recipe, following page.)

NS Tomato, Burrata and Arugula Salad

NICK STELLINO

Serves 4 to 6

1/4 teaspoon salt
1/4 teaspoon pepper
1/4 teaspoon onion powder
1/4 teaspoon dried oregano
1/4 teaspoon C&H® or Domino® sugar
4 large tomatoes, preferably heirloom
4 ounces baby arugula salad
3 tablespoons Pompeian® Extra Virgin Olive Oil, divided
1 tablespoon Pompeian® Balsamic Vinegar, divided
6 to 8 ounces burrata cheese, cut into 4 pieces, or fresh mozzarella, cut into slices
1 ounce shaved Parmesan cheese

Mix the dry spices and the sugar together in a small bowl. Cut the tomatoes into slices about 1/2 inch thick, place on a tray, and sprinkle with the spice mixture on each side. Let the slices rest and absorb the flavor for about 10 to 15 minutes. Dress the arugula salad with 1 1/2 tablespoons of the olive oil and 1/2 tablespoon of the vinegar.

TO SERVE:
Place the dressed salad in the middle of each plate; top with the tomato slices, then with the pieces of burrata or the fresh mozzarella slices. Drizzle each plate with the remaining oil and vinegar. Top the salads with shaved Parmesan, and serve.

“I have heard some Italians say, ‘I could never live too far from my fresh mozzarella.’ And I know they were not kidding!”

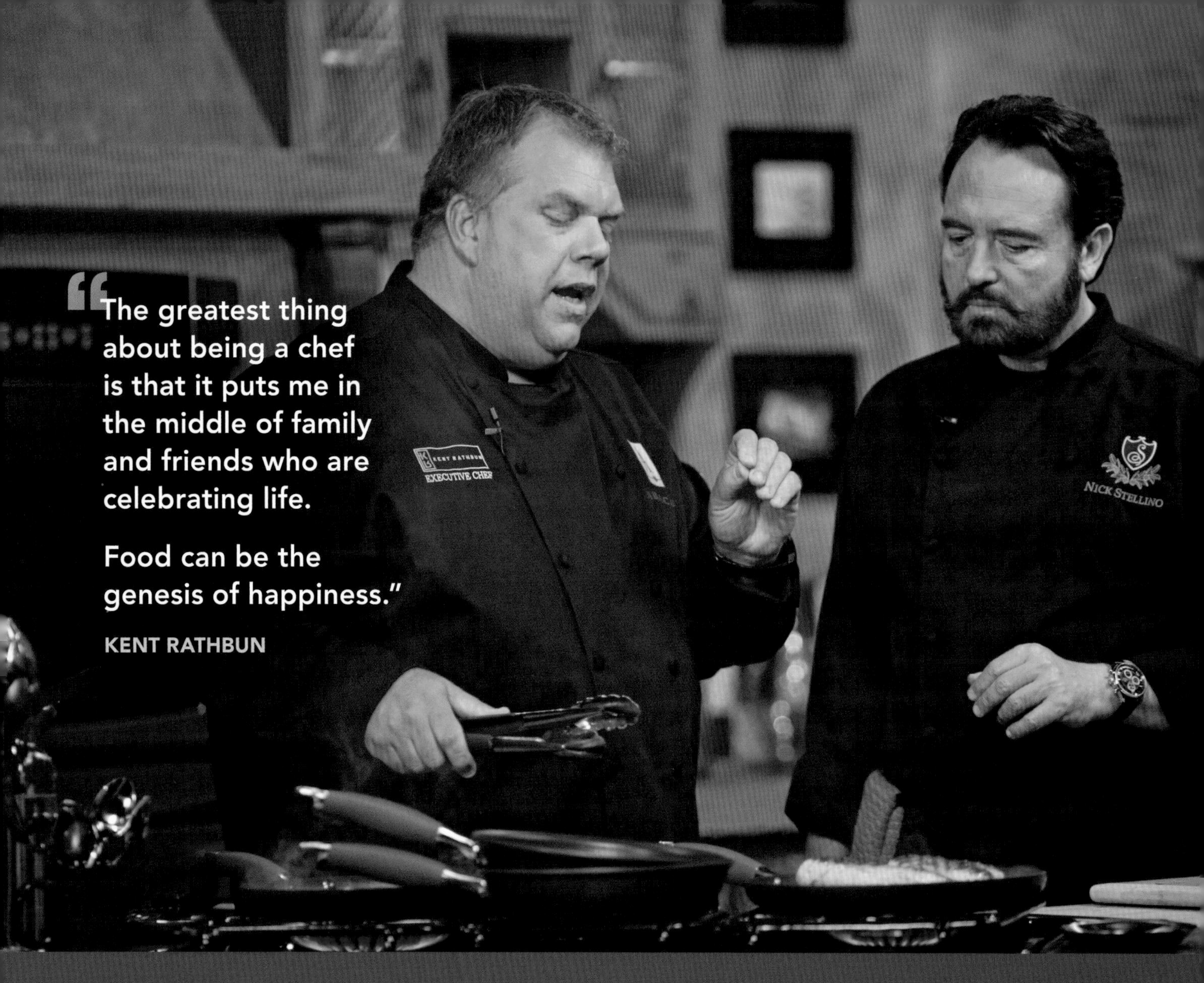

"The greatest thing about being a chef is that it puts me in the middle of family and friends who are celebrating life.

Food can be the genesis of happiness."

KENT RATHBUN

Chef Kent Rathbun

Abacus | Dallas ~ Jasper's Restaurants | Texas

Lobster Macaroni & Cheese with Truffle Oil

Jasper's Tomato, Grilled Asparagus and Blue Cheese Salad with Grilled Chicken

Wood-Grilled Pork Tenderloin with Peach Barbeque Sauce

Bourbon Creamed Corn

Dried Cherry-White Chocolate Bread Pudding

NS

Grilled Salad with Goat Cheese

Easy Chocolate Mousse

Lobster Macaroni & Cheese with Truffle Oil

KENT RATHBUN

Serves 8

4 ounces Pompeian® Extra Virgin Olive Oil, divided in half
2 tablespoons garlic, minced
2 tablespoons shallots, minced
24 ounces lobster meat, cubed
2 pounds orzo pasta, divided in half
2 quarts chicken stock, strained, divided in half
2 cups heavy cream
1 cup Romano cheese, grated
1/8 cup basil leaves, chiffonade
2 tablespoons oregano, chopped
2 tablespoons parsley, chopped
1/8 cup spinach leaves, chiffonade
8 ounces prosciutto ham, julienned thin
2 tablespoons cracked black pepper
2 tablespoons kosher salt
2 tablespoons Susan Rice™ Olive Oil with Summer Truffles

In a large pot over medium to high heat, sauté the garlic, shallots and lobster meat in 2 ounces extra virgin olive oil until the meat is medium-rare (about 2 minutes). Remove the lobster and set aside. The garlic and shallots may be left in the pot. Add the remaining 2 ounces olive oil to the pot. Lower the heat to medium and add half of the orzo pasta; sauté until golden brown. Add the remaining half of the pasta and cover with half of the chicken stock.

Continue cooking until the pasta absorbs most of the stock, then add the rest of the stock and continue cooking until all of the stock is absorbed.

Add the heavy cream and cheese, and stir until the cheese is melted. Add the chopped herbs and spinach.

In a sauté pan, quickly sauté the prosciutto ham until crisp. Incorporate the prosciutto into the pasta, then season with the cracked black pepper and kosher salt. Finish the dish with the lobster meat and truffle oil.

Jasper's Tomato, Grilled Asparagus and Blue Cheese Salad with Grilled Chicken

KENT RATHBUN

Serves 4

4 skinless, boneless chicken breasts, 8 ounces each
2 tablespoons Pompeian® Extra Light Olive Oil
1 tablespoon cracked black pepper
1 tablespoon kosher salt
32 slices tomato, ¼ inch thick (Tomatoes should be very fresh and very ripe.)
24 grilled asparagus spears (See accompanying recipe.)
4 ounces Maytag blue cheese, crumbled
12 red-onion rings, raw, for garnish
4 basil leaves, chiffonade, for garnish
8 ounces roast shallot-black pepper vinaigrette (See accompanying recipe.)

FOR THE GRILLED ASPARAGUS:

24 asparagus spears
2 tablespoons Pompeian® Extra Virgin Olive Oil
1 tablespoon cracked black pepper
1 tablespoon kosher salt

FOR THE ROAST SHALLOT-BLACK PEPPER VINAIGRETTE:

1 head garlic
2 small shallots
½ cup Pompeian® Extra Virgin Olive Oil, plus extra for brushing the garlic and shallots
2 tablespoons champagne vinegar or Pompeian® Pomegranate Infused Blush Balsamic Vinegar
2 tablespoons Pompeian® Balsamic Vinegar
1½ teaspoons cracked black pepper
1 teaspoon Worcestershire sauce
1½ teaspoons basil, chopped
1½ teaspoons chives, chopped
1½ teaspoons parsley, chopped
1½ teaspoons oregano, chopped
1½ teaspoons Susan Rice™ Olive Oil with Summer Truffles
1 tablespoon kosher salt

Coat the chicken breasts with the extra light olive oil and season with cracked black pepper and kosher salt. Grill on a charcoal grill or in a grill pan until the chicken is cooked through, approximately 5 to 7 minutes per side, depending on thickness. Remove the chicken breasts from the heat and slice each into 6 to 8 pieces.

TO PREPARE THE GRILLED ASPARAGUS:
Marinate the asparagus in the extra virgin olive oil and season with cracked black pepper and kosher salt. Grill over an open flame for 1 to 2 minutes. Remove from the heat and serve warm.

TO PREPARE THE ROAST SHALLOT-BLACK PEPPER VINAIGRETTE:
Cut off the top of the head of garlic and peel the shallots. To roast the garlic and shallots, brush with extra virgin olive oil and place in a baking dish in an oven preheated to 375 degrees. Roast until soft, approximately 35 to 40 minutes

In a medium bowl, mix ½ cup extra virgin olive oil and both vinegars. After the garlic and shallots cool, squeeze the garlic cloves out of their skins, and chop and mash them into a paste together with the shallots. Add the garlic-and-shallots paste to the rest of the ingredients, mix, and season with kosher salt.

TO SERVE:
On each plate lay out the tomato slices with the grilled asparagus in a nice arrangement. Arrange the slices of chicken breast on the plate next to the tomatoes. Sprinkle the Maytag blue cheese over the top of the salad, and garnish with the red-onion rings and basil. Drizzle 2 ounces of the vinaigrette over each salad.

Wood-Grilled Pork Tenderloin with Peach Barbeque Sauce

KENT RATHBUN

Serves 8

FOR THE PEACH BARBEQUE SAUCE:

8 ounces smoked bacon, diced (1 ham hock may be substituted.)
1 cup onion (smoked or grilled), **coarsely chopped**
2 tablespoons garlic cloves (smoked or grilled), **chopped**
2 arbol chiles, stems removed
2 cups peaches (fresh or dried), **coarsely chopped**
1 tablespoon cracked black pepper
2 tablespoons Worcestershire sauce
2 cups fresh orange juice
2 cups ketchup
6 dashes Tabasco sauce
2 tablespoons fresh lemon juice
2 teaspoons kosher salt

FOR THE PORK TENDERLOIN:

8 pieces pork tenderloin (about 8 ounces each), **trimmed of fat and silverskin**
3 ounces Pompeian® Extra Virgin Olive Oil
2 tablespoons cracked black pepper
2 tablespoons kosher salt
1 tablespoon granulated garlic

TO PREPARE THE PEACH BARBEQUE SAUCE:

Place the bacon in a small sauce pot and start cooking on medium heat until crisp, then add the onions and garlic, and sauté until caramelized. Add the arbol chiles and continue to cook until they start to toast. Add the peaches and cracked black pepper, and deglaze with the Worcestershire sauce and orange juice.

Reduce the orange juice until it starts to thicken. Add the ketchup and reduce the heat to low. Continue cooking for about 15 minutes. Season with the Tabasco sauce, lemon juice and salt. Strain the barbeque sauce and set aside.

TO PREPARE THE PORK TENDERLOIN:

On a sheet pan, rub the tenderloins with the olive oil and season with the cracked black pepper, kosher salt and granulated garlic. Grill over an open flame or on a charbroiler until the desired temperature is reached. (Medium-rare is best.)

TO SERVE:

Serve the tenderloins, sliced, with bourbon creamed corn, and finish with the barbeque sauce.

Bourbon Creamed Corn

KENT RATHBUN

Serves 8

2 ounces whole butter
2 tablespoons garlic cloves, minced
2 tablespoons shallots, minced
3 cups fresh corn kernels
2 ounces red bell pepper, stem and seeds removed, diced small
2 ounces bourbon
1 cup heavy cream
¼ cup green onions, chopped
1 tablespoon cracked black pepper
1 tablespoon kosher salt

In a large sauté pan, over medium heat, add the whole butter, and sauté the garlic and shallots until translucent. Add the corn kernels and bell pepper, and continue cooking for 2 minutes.

Deglaze with the bourbon and add the cream. Reduce until the cream starts to thicken.

Finish with the green onions, cracked black pepper and kosher salt.

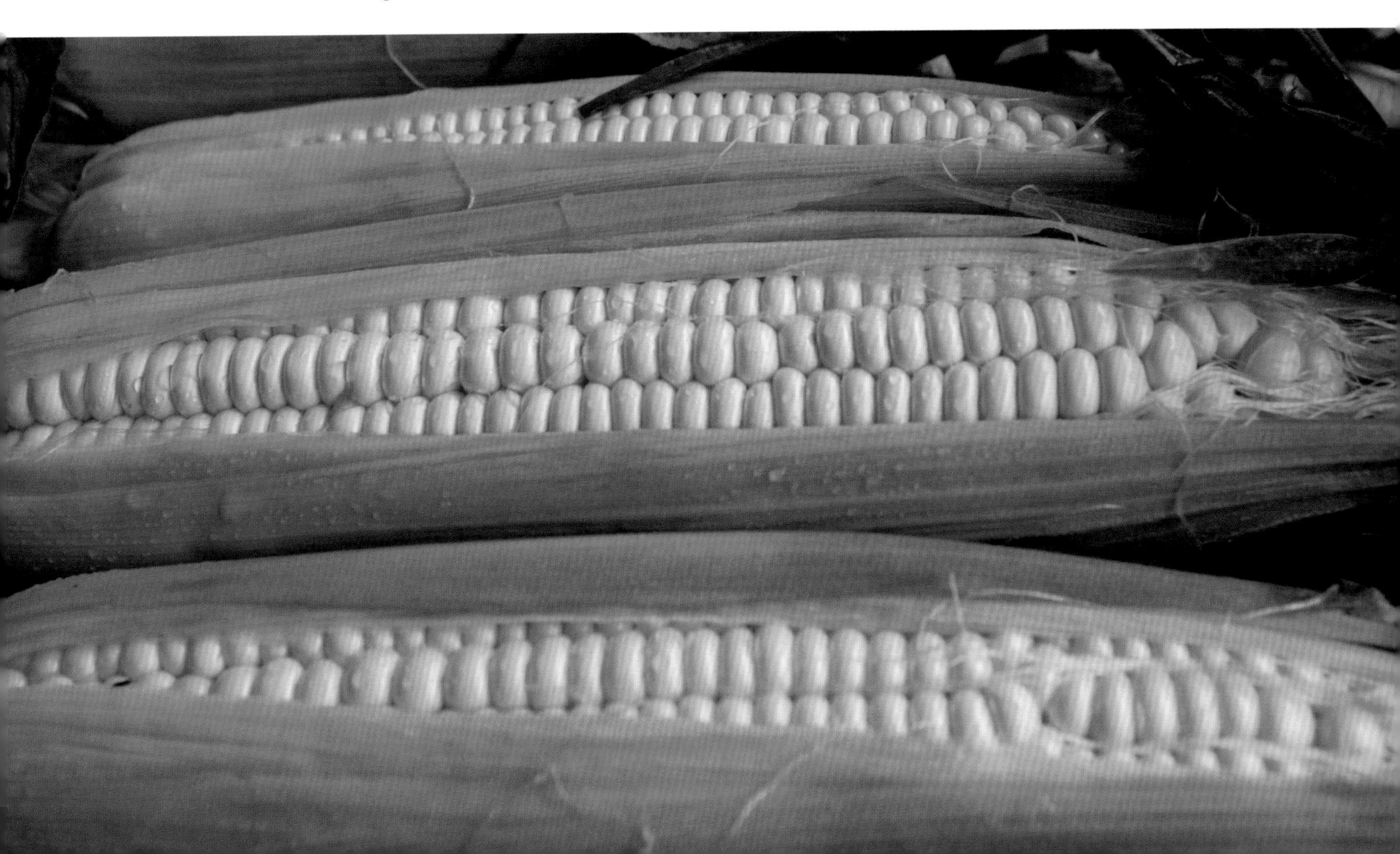

Dried Cherry-White Chocolate Bread Pudding

KENT RATHBUN

Serves 8

1 18-inch baguette
8 ounces white chocolate, chopped
8 ounces dried cherries
1 cup C&H® or Domino® sugar
1 tablespoon cinnamon
1 teaspoon nutmeg
6 large eggs
2 cups heavy cream
2 cups milk
1 tablespoon vanilla extract
4 ounces butter, sliced
1 4-ounce jar cherry jelly

Cut the baguette into 1-inch pieces and transfer to a large mixing bowl. Add in the white chocolate and dried cherries. In a separate mixing bowl, mix together the sugar, cinnamon and nutmeg. Set aside about ¼ cup of this mixture for later.

Add to the sugar mixture the eggs, cream, milk and vanilla, and mix thoroughly. Pour the custard over the bread, and mix. Transfer to a large baking pan. Sprinkle with the remaining sugar mixture, evenly place the butter slices on top, and bake at 325 degrees until golden brown, approximately 45 to 55 minutes. Remove from the oven, spread cherry jelly evenly on top, and serve.

"I know that the concept of a grilled salad might be difficult to grasp at first, but after your first bite, it will soon become your favorite kind of salad, especially in summertime, when you will be hosting your own family barbecues!"

NS

Grilled Salad with Goat Cheese

NICK STELLINO

Serves 4 to 6

2 large heads radicchio di Treviso, cut in half
2 large heads Belgian endive, cut in half
2 red bell peppers, cut in quarters and seeded
2 yellow bell peppers, cut in quarters and seeded
6 tablespoons Pompeian® Extra Virgin Olive Oil, divided
5 ounces baby arugula salad
8 tablespoons goat cheese, crumbled
1½ tablespoons Pompeian® Balsamic Vinegar

Preheat the broiler to high.

Brush the radicchio, endive and peppers with 4 tablespoons olive oil. Cook on a hot barbecue or under the broiler for 2 to 3 minutes per side, until they start to color on each side. Place on a cutting board while still hot and cut into 1-inch pieces. Place the arugula salad and the goat cheese in a bowl with the radicchio, endive and peppers, and mix well until the cheese starts to melt.
Add the remaining 2 tablespoons olive oil and the balsamic vinegar, mix well, and serve.

NS

Easy Chocolate Mousse

NICK STELLINO

Serves 4 to 6

1 cup semisweet chocolate morsels (6 ounces)
3 cups heavy cream, divided
2 tablespoons C&H® or Domino® sugar

Melt the chocolate morsels in the top of a double boiler. Whisk in 1 cup heavy cream until well blended. Remove from the heat. Let sit for 20 to 30 minutes until the mixture has reached room temperature.

In a large, chilled mixing bowl, combine the remaining 2 cups cream and the sugar. Use a hand-held or electric mixer to whip them together until stiff peaks form when the beaters are stopped and lifted out.

Gently fold half of the melted chocolate mixture into the whipped cream. Add the second half, and fold in gently. If the mousse becomes soft, it's no cause for alarm. Chill in a bowl for 15 to 20 minutes, and it will be as good as new.

Serve family-style, in a big bowl, with your favorite kind of whipped cream on the side.

CHEF'S TIP: For a more elegant presentation, fill a pastry bag equipped with a star tip with the mousse and pipe it into individual bowls or glasses. Sprinkle with grated white or dark chocolate, and top with sweet whipped cream.

> "I think food and wine always bring people together. Some of my best memories are of times spent with friends and family around the dinner table."
>
> **HEATHER TERHUNE**

Chef Heather Terhune

Atwood Café | Chicago

Maryland Crab Fritters with Herb Salad and Lemon Aïoli

Grilled Arctic Char with Chipotle Barbecue Sauce, Jicama Salad & Mango-Pineapple Salsa

NS Tuna Tartare with Grilled Toast

Maryland Crab Fritters with Herb Salad and Lemon Aïoli

HEATHER TERHUNE

Serves 4

FOR THE LEMON AÏOLI:

½ cup mayonnaise
Juice and zest of 1 lemon
1½ teaspoons Dijon mustard
1 teaspoon sherry wine vinegar
¼ cup Pompeian® Extra Virgin Olive Oil
Salt and pepper to taste

FOR THE CRAB FRITTERS:

2 large eggs, separated
1 tablespoon crème fraîche or sour cream
1 cup (about 6 ounces) **packed Maryland backfin crabmeat** (no claw meat)
2 tablespoons finely chopped fresh chives
1 tablespoon finely chopped shallots
1 tablespoon chopped Italian parsley
1 tablespoon butter, for sautéing
Salt and pepper

FOR THE HERB SALAD:

2 tablespoons Pompeian® Extra Virgin Olive Oil
1 tablespoon lemon juice
Salt and pepper
½ cup (packed) **fresh basil leaves**
½ cup (packed) **fresh Italian parsley leaves**

TO PREPARE THE LEMON AÏOLI:

Place the mayonnaise in a small bowl. Whisk in the lemon juice, zest, mustard and vinegar.

Gradually whisk in the olive oil. Season with salt and pepper to taste.

TO PREPARE THE CRAB FRITTERS:

Whisk the egg yolks and crème fraîche in a small bowl. Combine the crabmeat, chives, shallots and parsley in a medium bowl. Gently add the yolk mixture to the crabmeat.

Beat the egg whites in a bowl until stiff but not dry; gently fold into the crab mixture. Melt the butter in a large nonstick sauté pan over medium heat. For each fritter, drop a quarter of the crab mixture (about ½ cup) into the pan, spacing the mounds apart. Season with salt and pepper, and flatten slightly.

Cook the fritters until the bottoms are brown, about 3 minutes. Turn the fritters over. Cook until they are cooked through and brown on this side as well, about 3 minutes longer.

TO PREPARE THE HERB SALAD:
While the fritters are cooking, whisk the olive oil and lemon juice in a medium bowl to blend. Season with salt and pepper. Mix in the herbs.

TO SERVE:
Place a crab fritter on each plate. Top each fritter with a dollop of lemon aïoli and place the herb salad alongside it.

Grilled Arctic Char with Chipotle Barbecue Sauce, Jicama Salad & Mango-Pineapple Salsa

HEATHER TERHUNE

Serves 6

FOR THE CHIPOTLE BARBECUE SAUCE (yields 3 cups):

1 tablespoon Pompeian® Extra Virgin Olive Oil
1 small onion, finely chopped
4 garlic cloves, minced
1 tablespoon dry mustard powder
1 teaspoon red pepper flakes
3 tablespoons C&H® or Domino® dark brown sugar
2 cups ketchup
3 whole chipotles in adobo sauce, finely chopped
1/3 cup Worcestershire sauce
1/3 cup cider vinegar
1 tablespoon molasses
1/4 teaspoon freshly ground black pepper

FOR THE JICAMA SALAD (6 servings):

1 large jicama, peeled and cut into thin matchstick slices
2 large carrots, peeled and cut into thin matchstick slices
1 red bell pepper, cut into thin matchstick slices
1/2 cup radishes, sliced
1 small red onion, peeled, julienned
Juice of 3 limes (no zest)
2 tablespoons cider vinegar
1/2 teaspoon cayenne pepper
2 tablespoons honey
1/4 cup canola oil
1/4 cup fresh cilantro, finely minced
1/4 cup fresh green onion, sliced
Kosher salt and freshly ground black pepper to taste

FOR THE MANGO-PINEAPPLE SALSA (6 servings):

2 cups fresh pineapple, cut into 1/4-inch dice
1 ripe mango, peeled and pitted, cut into 1/4-inch dice
1 red bell pepper, seeded, cut into 1/4-inch dice
1/2 cup English hothouse cucumber, seeded, cut into 1/4-inch dice
1/2 cup red onion, cut into 1/4-inch dice
3 tablespoons fresh cilantro, minced

2 tablespoons fresh mint, minced
2 tablespoons jalapeño, seeded and minced
2 tablespoons freshly squeezed lime juice
Salt and freshly ground black pepper to taste

FOR THE GRILLED ARCTIC CHAR (6 servings)**:**
6 6-ounce Arctic char fillets, skin on, scaled (You can substitute wild salmon or trout.)
2 tablespoons Pompeian® Extra Light Olive Oil
Salt and pepper
Chipotle barbecue sauce (See accompanying recipe.)
Jicama salad (See accompanying recipe.)
Mango-pineapple salsa (See accompanying recipe.)

TO PREPARE THE CHIPOTLE BARBECUE SAUCE:
In a saucepan, heat the extra virgin olive oil over medium heat. Add the onion and garlic; cook, stirring occasionally, until translucent, about 5 minutes. Stir in the mustard powder and red pepper flakes; cook 30 seconds. Reduce the heat to low; stir in the brown sugar, ketchup, chipotles, Worcestershire sauce, vinegar, molasses and black pepper. Cook, stirring occasionally, until thickened, 5 to 10 minutes.

TO PREPARE THE JICAMA SALAD:
Use a vegetable peeler to peel the jicama. Cut into thin matchstick slices, using a Japanese mandoline or the shredding blade of a food processor. Use this method for the carrots as well. Place the jicama, carrots, red bell pepper, radishes and red onion in a large bowl. In a small bowl, whisk together the lime juice, vinegar, cayenne pepper, honey and canola oil. Stir in the cilantro and green onions, and season with salt and pepper. Pour over the jicama salad. Allow the flavors to marinate for about 15 minutes at room temperature before serving.

TO PREPARE THE MANGO-PINEAPPLE SALSA:
Combine the ingredients in a medium-sized bowl; toss to blend. Season the salsa with salt and pepper. Refrigerate to blend the flavors, at least 1 hour and up to 24 hours.

TO PREPARE THE GRILLED ARCTIC CHAR:
Prepare a charcoal or gas grill, bringing it to medium-high heat, or use a hot grill pan. Brush the fish with the extra light olive oil; sprinkle with salt and pepper. Grill just until opaque in the center, about 5 minutes per side. Brush with barbecue sauce before each turn.

TO SERVE:
Divide the jicama salad among 6 plates. Place 1 fish fillet on top of each salad. Top with mango-pineapple salsa and extra barbecue sauce if desired.

NS Tuna Tartare with Grilled Toast

NICK STELLINO

Makes 4 entrée servings or 6 appetizers

FOR THE GRILLED TOAST:

14 ½-inch-thick slices country French bread
2 tablespoons Pompeian® Extra Virgin Olive Oil

FOR THE TUNA TARTARE:

1 pound fresh tuna (sashimi grade), **cut into approximately ¼-inch dice**
2 tablespoons pear, peeled and diced (approximately half a pear)
2 tablespoons garlic, finely chopped
3 tablespoons toasted pine nuts
1 teaspoon lemon zest, chopped (approximately 1 lemon)
1 jalapeño pepper, seeded and chopped
2 tablespoons sundried tomatoes packed in olive oil, each tomato chopped into approximately 4 equal pieces
1 tablespoon mint, chopped
1 tablespoon basil, chopped
1 tablespoon parsley, chopped
½ teaspoon salt (or more to taste)
1 tablespoon sesame oil
3 tablespoons Pompeian® Extra Virgin Olive Oil
1 large egg yolk
½ teaspoon Worcestershire sauce

3 tablespoons Pompeian® Extra Virgin Olive Oil (optional)
2 tablespoons Pompeian® Balsamic Vinegar (optional)

TO PREPARE THE GRILLED TOAST:

Brush the sliced bread with 2 tablespoons olive oil, and toast in the oven under the broiler or grill on the barbecue until toasted, about 1 minute per side.

TO PREPARE THE TUNA TARTARE:

Mix the tuna and all of the other ingredients in a stainless steel bowl, stirring well to incorporate the flavors. (This should not be done until right before you are ready to serve the tartare.) Taste, and adjust the salt to your liking.

TO SERVE:
For each entrée-size serving, place the tuna mixture into a 3-inch cookie-cutter ring about 2 inches deep, pushing firmly to give the mixture a compact consistency. Carefully lift the ring off; the tuna will stay in the shape of a small cylinder in the center of the plate. Serve with slices of grilled toast. Make extra toast; your guests will ask for more!

OPTIONAL: For a more elegant look, decorate the perimeter of the plate with a drizzle of olive oil and balsamic vinegar.

Chef Elise Wiggins

Panzano | Denver

Fried Palisade Peach Pie with Vanilla Gelato

Palisade Peach Salad with Crispy Prosciutto-Crusted Goat Cheese Balls & Hazelnut-Mint Vinaigrette

Mushroom Crêpes with Fonduta Sauce

Chocolate and Cherry Cake

NS

Pork Chops with Nancibella Sauce

Spinach Salad with Feta Cheese and Seedless Grapes

Fried Palisade Peach Pie with Vanilla Gelato

ELISE WIGGINS

Makes 8 pies

FOR THE FILLING:

1 cup C&H® or Domino® sugar
4 cups fresh (or frozen and thawed) **Palisade peach slices, peeled**
(Palisade peaches are grown on the Western Slope of Colorado and are prized for their sweetness. Substituting everyday peaches will work, too.)
4 whole cloves
¼ teaspoon freshly grated nutmeg
2 tablespoons fresh lemon juice
¼ cup cornstarch
Vanilla bean gelato, for serving

FOR THE CRUST:

2 cups all-purpose flour, plus extra for dusting the work surface
3 tablespoons C&H® or Domino® sugar, plus extra for sprinkling the pies
1¼ teaspoons ground cinnamon
½ teaspoon salt
4 tablespoons cream cheese, diced and chilled
9 tablespoons solid vegetable shortening, chilled, plus more for frying
4 to 6 tablespoons ice water

TO PREPARE THE FILLING:

In a large saucepan over medium heat, combine the sugar, peach slices, cloves and nutmeg. Mix until blended. Bring the mixture to a boil; turn down the heat and allow the mixture to simmer until the peaches are softened, 20 to 25 minutes. Using a slotted spoon, remove the peaches from the saucepan and place in a small bowl. Reserve ⅓ cup plus 2 tablespoons of the peach liquid in the saucepan and discard the rest. Return the peaches to the saucepan.

In a small bowl, combine the lemon juice and cornstarch. Whisk the cornstarch mixture into the peach mixture, stirring until combined. Bring the mixture to a boil and cook for 1 minute, stirring constantly to keep it from sticking; the mixture will be very thick. Transfer the peach mixture to a clean bowl and chill for 1 hour, or until completely chilled.

TO PREPARE THE CRUST:

Sift the flour, sugar, cinnamon and salt together into a large mixing bowl. Add the chilled cream cheese and shortening, and—working with your hands or a fork—mix until the mixture resembles coarse meal. Add the cold water, 1 tablespoon at a time, and gently mix until the dough begins to stick together. Form the dough into a round disk, cover with plastic wrap, and refrigerate for 30 minutes.

Remove the dough from the refrigerator and divide it into 8 equal portions. On a lightly floured surface, roll out each dough piece into a thin circle about 6 inches in diameter. Place ¼ cup of the chilled peach filling into the center of each dough round. Fold the dough over, making a half-moon-shaped pastry; trim any excess dough, leaving a ½-inch edge around the filling, and crimp the edges together with a fork. Chill the pies for 30 minutes.

In a large, heavy skillet, melt the extra vegetable shortening to a depth of about ½ inch. Heat the shortening to 350 degrees. Meanwhile, line a baking sheet with paper towels and sprinkle some of the extra sugar lightly over the paper towels. Fry the pies in the skillet, in batches, until golden brown on both sides, about 2 minutes on each side. Transfer to the paper-towel-lined baking sheet and sprinkle the tops of the pies with sugar.

Serve immediately with vanilla bean gelato. Enjoy.

Palisade Peach Salad with Prosciutto-Crusted Goat Cheese Balls & Hazelnut-Mint Vinaigrette

ELISE WIGGINS

Serves 4

½ cup hazelnut-mint vinaigrette (See accompanying recipe.)
4 Palisade peaches, pitted, skins removed, each peach cut into 4 wedges
Goat cheese balls (See accompanying recipe.)
2 tablespoons High Country Orchards Rainier cherries, pitted and halved, for garnish
1 cup watercress (just the leafy tops), **for garnish**

FOR THE HAZELNUT-MINT VINAIGRETTE:
1 cup fresh mint leaves
1 shallot, finely chopped
1 tablespoon garlic, freshly chopped
2 tablespoons honey
1 tablespoon sea salt
½ cup Pompeian® Extra Virgin Olive Oil
¼ cup hazelnut oil
¼ cup Pompeian® Red Wine Vinegar
¼ cup roasted hazelnuts, roughly chopped

FOR THE GOAT CHEESE BALLS:
¼ cup Haystack Mountain Herbes de Provence Chèvre (or your favorite chèvre)
2 tablespoons cherry jam
2 ounces shaved prosciutto, fried until crisp and then crumbled into crumbs suitable for crusting

TO PREPARE THE HAZELNUT-MINT VINAIGRETTE:
Combine the mint, shallots, garlic, honey, salt and oils in a blender. Blend together until the mint is nicely chopped. Pour into a container and add the vinegar and chopped hazelnuts. Allow the flavors to infuse at room temperature for at least 1 hour, or store overnight in the refrigerator.

TO PREPARE THE GOAT CHEESE BALLS:
Roll a tablespoon of goat cheese into a ball. Continue with this until all the goat cheese is used. Heat the cherry jam with a tablespoon of water until just melted. Pour over the goat cheese balls. Roll the balls around until completely covered with the jam. Then roll the balls in the prosciutto crumbs. They should be well crusted.

TO SERVE:

Divide the vinaigrette among 4 plates. It should thinly cover the bottom of each plate and should be a nice bright green color. Place 4 peach wedges on each plate. Make sure there is space in between the wedges. Place a goat cheese ball in between each peach wedge. Garnish with cherries and watercress. The end result should be a colorful plate of green, orangey pink and red.

Mushroom Crêpes with Fonduta Sauce

ELISE WIGGINS

Makes 4 servings

FOR THE CRÊPES:

½ cup flour
1 egg
⅔ cup milk
1 tablespoon butter, melted

FOR THE FONDUTA SAUCE:

1 tablespoon Pompeian® Extra Virgin Olive Oil
½ shallot, diced
1 teaspoon garlic, chopped
¼ cup white wine
¼ cup chicken stock
1 cup heavy cream
1 ounce fontina, grated
1 ounce Gorgonzola, grated
1 ounce Parmigiano-Reggiano, grated

FOR THE MUSHROOM FILLING:

1 tablespoon unsalted butter
1 tablespoon Pompeian® Extra Virgin Olive Oil, plus extra for searing the filled crêpes
1 cup mixed wild mushrooms, sliced ¼ inch thick
(We choose the type of mushroom according to the season.)
2 teaspoons garlic, chopped
2 teaspoons fresh thyme leaves, picked off the woody stem and chopped
1 teaspoon sea salt

4 teaspoons Susan Rice™ Black Winter Truffle Olive Oil

TO PREPARE THE CRÊPES:

Make the crêpes first. Combine all of the ingredients. Allow to rest for 1 hour. Spray a non-stick crêpe or egg pan with pan spray. Take a 2-ounce ladle and pour the batter into the pan. Roll the batter around until it creates a perfect circle. Let cook until you see the edges curl and the crêpe slides around freely. Then flip to quickly set the other side. Place on a plate. Shingle the crêpes as you go.

TO PREPARE THE FONDUTA SAUCE:
In a sauté pan, heat the olive oil. Add the shallots and garlic. Cook on a low temperature or flame. Once translucent, add the wine and chicken stock. Reduce by half. Add the cream. Heat to a boil. Slowly add the cheese until all is incorporated. Reduce until slightly thick.

TO PREPARE THE MUSHROOM FILLING:
Heat up a sauté pan with the butter and olive oil. Add the mushrooms, garlic and thyme. Once tender, add the salt. Then place a small portion of filling in a crêpe. Roll up and set seam side down.

Heat up a sauté pan again with a little olive oil. Sear your crêpe, seam side down first. Then flip and toast the other side. Place on a plate and pour fonduta sauce over the top.

Lastly, drizzle truffle oil over the crêpes, and serve.

Chocolate and Cherry Cake

ELISE WIGGINS

Serves 6

½ pound bittersweet chocolate, preferably organic
½ pound butter
1 cup C&H® or Domino® sugar, divided
½ cup milk
6 eggs
6 egg yolks
½ cup dried cherries
2 cups water
Fresh cherries with stems, for garnish
Fresh Cherry Jubilee, for serving (See accompanying recipe.)
Real vanilla bean gelato or vanilla ice cream, for serving

FOR THE CHERRY JUBILEE:
½ cup C&H® or Domino® sugar
1 tablespoon cornstarch
¼ cup each water and orange juice
3 cups pitted fresh, sweet cherries
½ teaspoon grated orange peel
¼ cup brandy (optional)

Melt the chocolate and butter in a double boiler. Heat ½ cup sugar and the milk together until they come to a boil; stir into the melted chocolate and butter. Allow the mixture to cool. In a separate bowl, stir together the eggs and egg yolks. Stir the eggs into the chocolate mixture.

Mix the dried cherries, the water and the remaining ½ cup sugar together in a small pot and simmer until the cherries have rehydrated and the liquid reduces to a thin syrup, about 15 to 20 minutes. Combine the cherry mixture with the chocolate mixture.

Butter 6 4-ounce ramekins and line them with paper; portion the chocolate cake into each ramekin. Place several cherries on top of each cake and bake for 30 minutes at 300 degrees.

TO PREPARE THE CHERRY JUBILEE (recipe may be halved):
Combine the sugar and cornstarch. Blend in the water and orange juice, and bring to a boil. Cook and stir until thickened and smooth. Add the cherries and orange peel; return to the boil and simmer 10 minutes. Gently heat the brandy, pour over the sauce, and flame, if desired. The Jubilee can also be used by itself as a topping over vanilla ice cream.

TO SERVE:
When the cakes have cooled enough to handle, unmold each and place in a serving dish. Top with some of the Cherry Jubilee and a dollop of softened ice cream or gelato.

"Here is an easy technique to make every pork chop you cook from now on tender and full of flavor. You are going to owe me big-time for the secret of my little brine: water, sugar and salt. Can you believe how simple this is?"

NS

Pork Chops with Nancibella Sauce

NICK STELLINO

Serves 4

4 pork chops, bone-in, center-cut, totaling 2 to 2½ pounds
Salt and pepper to taste
3 tablespoons Pompeian® Extra Light Olive Oil
3 tablespoons softened butter (optional)

FOR THE BRINE:
2 cups water
2 tablespoons C&H® or Domino® sugar
1 tablespoon salt

FOR THE NANCIBELLA SAUCE:
4 tablespoons Pompeian® Extra Virgin Olive Oil
¼ teaspoon red pepper flakes (optional)
1 medium white onion, finely chopped, or 5 small shallots, peeled and finely chopped
2 tablespoons fresh parsley, chopped
2 tablespoons fresh thyme leaves, loosely packed
2 garlic cloves, finely chopped
1 cup sherry
¼ cup grenadine syrup
1 tablespoon Worcestershire sauce
4 cups chicken stock
Salt and pepper to taste

Place the pork chops in a resealable plastic bag. Place the water, sugar and salt in a small bowl, stir well to incorporate, and pour over the pork chops in the bag. Seal the bag shut and brine the pork chops for at least 5 hours or preferably overnight.

Make the Nancibella Sauce (see accompanying recipe) and keep warm.

Preheat the barbecue. If using a gas model, set all the burners to high and close the cover until the internal temperature reaches 500 degrees.

Take the chops out of the brine and pat dry with a paper towel. Discard the brine. Sprinkle the chops with salt and pepper to taste. Brush each side of the pork chops with the extra light olive oil. You do not need to use all of it.

Reduce the heat on the grill to medium and cook the chops for 3 to 4 minutes per side with the cover down. (Alternatively, you can cook the chops in a hot sauté pan with 1 tablespoon extra light olive oil over medium-high heat for 3 to 4 minutes per side.) Place the chops on a tray and cover with foil.

Bring the Nancibella Sauce to a boil in a saucepan large enough to hold all of the chops. Add the chops and reduce the heat to a simmer. Cook the chops, basting them with the sauce, for 2 to 3 more minutes over medium-low heat. Place each chop in an individual serving dish. Bring the sauce to a boil over high heat, and cook for 1 to 2 more minutes until it thickens to the desired consistency. Add the optional butter, swirling it in the pan until it melts completely. Pour the Nancibella Sauce over the chops and serve. Sautéed green beans make a perfect accompaniment.

TO PREPARE THE NANCIBELLA SAUCE:
Pour the extra virgin olive oil into a large saucepan and cook over high heat until it starts to sizzle. Add the optional red pepper flakes, the white onion and the fresh herbs; reduce the heat to medium and cook, stirring well, for 3 to 4 minutes until the onion starts to soften. Add the garlic and cook for 1 more minute, stirring well.

Add the sherry, grenadine and Worcestershire sauce, and increase the heat to high. Stir well until reduced by two-thirds, about 3 to 4 minutes. Add the chicken stock, bring to a boil, and cover. Reduce the heat to low and cook for 40 minutes.

Strain the sauce through a fine sieve, pushing the pulp through with a rubber spatula and trying to extract as much liquid as possible.

Bring the strained sauce to a boil over high heat. Reduce the heat to medium and cook for 8 to 10 minutes until the liquid reduces by about one-third and reaches a thick consistency. Add salt and pepper to taste. Keep warm until ready to use, or store, covered, in the refrigerator once it cools down. The sauce can be made up to 2 days ahead.

"Make friends with your butcher; he will make your life taste a whole lot better! There is a lot we need to learn about meat, and if you are willing to learn, he is willing to teach you."

NS Spinach Salad with Feta Cheese and Seedless Grapes

NICK STELLINO

Serves 4

FOR THE DRESSING:

8 cherry tomatoes
1 tablespoon chopped parsley
¼ teaspoon salt
4 tablespoons Pompeian® Pomegranate Infused Balsamic Vinegar
1 tablespoon feta cheese, crumbled
1 tablespoon C&H® or Domino® sugar
6 tablespoons Pompeian® Extra Virgin Olive Oil

FOR THE SALAD:

7 ounces baby spinach leaves
5 tablespoons toasted pine nuts
1 cup red seedless grapes, cut in half
5 tablespoons feta cheese, crumbled

TO PREPARE THE DRESSING:

Place all of the ingredients except the olive oil in a food processor and process for about 30 seconds. Add the oil in a thin stream until it is all incorporated into the dressing. Turn off the processor, transfer the dressing to a bowl, and put aside until you are ready to dress the salad.

TO PREPARE THE SALAD:

In a large bowl, mix the spinach leaves, pine nuts and seedless grapes, and toss with the dressing. Divide the mixture among 4 plates, sprinkle with the crumbled feta cheese, and serve.

"My philosophy of life and cooking has always been to make the most of what you have.

I aspire to develop the vices and the spices in my life and the flavors in my food."

PATRICIA WILLIAMS

Chef Patricia Williams

District | New York

Watercress Salad with Poached Pears & Gorgonzola

Split Pea Chowder

Slow-Roasted Breast of Veal

Claufouti

NS

Tuna Steaks with Peperonata Sauce

Pears in Red Wine Sauce

Watercress Salad with Poached Pears & Gorgonzola

PATRICIA WILLIAMS

Serves 6

FOR THE POACHED PEARS:

6 Seckel pears, or 3 large pears cut in half lengthwise
2 cups red wine
½ cup C&H® or Domino® sugar
1 stick of cinnamon
4 cloves
1 cup water

FOR THE VINAIGRETTE:

1 egg yolk
1 egg
4 tablespoons Dijon mustard
2 cloves garlic, cooked until soft
⅓ cup lemon juice
2 cups Pompeian® Extra Virgin Olive Oil
Salt and pepper to taste
½ cup heavy cream

FOR THE WATERCRESS SALAD:

3 bunches watercress, cleaned of large stems and washed
Salt and pepper
¼ pound Gorgonzola

TO PREPARE THE POACHED PEARS:

Peel the pears and place in water. Bring the wine, sugar, cinnamon stick, cloves and 1 cup water to a boil and add the pears. Turn the heat to a simmer and cook the pears until a small knife can pierce them easily. Do not overcook; there should still be some texture to the pears. Remove from the stove and let cool in the liquid. The pears can be made 3 days in advance.

TO PREPARE THE VINAIGRETTE:

Place all of the ingredients except the oil, salt and pepper and cream in a blender or Robot Coupe food processor. Blend, then slowly add the oil. Season to taste with salt and pepper, add the cream, then blend again. This is too much dressing for the 6 salads but will keep in the refrigerator, covered, for 1 week.

TO ASSEMBLE THE SALAD:

Place a pear (or, if using 3 large pears, a pear half) on each plate. Dress the watercress with the vinaigrette, season with salt and pepper, and place on the plate alongside the pear. Crumble the Gorgonzola over each salad.

Split Pea Chowder

PATRICIA WILLIAMS

Serves 6

5 slices bacon (Save the drippings.)
2 onions, diced
1 tablespoon garlic, finely chopped
3 quarts homemade or store-bought chicken stock
½ pound whole pigeon peas (Goya® brand), **soaked overnight**
½ pound green split peas
2 cups carrots, diced
2 cups potatoes, diced

Cook the bacon over medium heat until crispy, then chop it into small pieces and reserve. In a separate pan on medium heat, sauté the onions for about 8 minutes in the drippings from the bacon. Add the garlic and the cooked bacon pieces to the sautéed onions; cook over medium heat until the onions and garlic are soft but not browned, about 10 minutes. Place the chicken stock and whole pigeon peas in a large pot along with the bacon, garlic and onions, and cook over low heat until the peas are almost tender, about 35 minutes. Add the split peas and cook for about 15 minutes until almost tender, then add the carrots and potatoes. Cook for approximately 10 more minutes. The soup is ready when the carrots and potatoes are done.

"Sometimes at night, when I am cleaning up in the kitchen after dinner, I find beauty in the small details of my surroundings, such as my cooking tools, which I think of as musical instruments resting before the next symphony."

Slow-Roasted Breast of Veal

PATRICIA WILLIAMS

Serves 6

Breast of veal (Ask the butcher for a breast of veal weighing about 5 pounds. My neighborhood supermarket usually has one.)
6 cloves garlic
½ bunch thyme

FOR THE RUB FOR THE VEAL:
1 cup salt
2 cups C&H® Golden Brown or Domino® Light Brown sugar
2 tablespoons cinnamon
2 tablespoons red pepper flakes

One to two days before cooking the veal, mix together the ingredients for the rub and coat the meat with it.

When you are ready to roast the veal, wrap it in aluminum foil with 6 cloves of garlic and ½ bunch of thyme. Roast the veal for 3 hours at 250 degrees.

I love this recipe because it allows you time to be with family and friends. You may cook the veal two days before and just reheat.

Claufouti

PATRICIA WILLIAMS

Serves 6

A complicated name for a very simple dessert.

3½ ounces butter
1½ ounces C&H® Powdered Sugar or Domino® Confectioners Sugar
1¾ cups almond flour or finely ground almonds (If using almonds, make sure that you do not make almond butter. Add 1 tablespoon flour to the almonds and chop finely in a food processor.)
1 pinch salt
2 eggs
¼ cup heavy cream
Nonstick cooking spray, such as PAM®
2 cups fruit of your choice (I use whatever is in season.)
Whipped cream or ice cream, for serving

Cream together the butter and sugar. Beat in the almond flour and a pinch of salt. Whisk together the eggs and cream, mix in with the flour mixture, and pour into a 9-inch quiche or pie plate that has been sprayed with PAM®. Place the fruit on top of the egg-and-flour mixture and bake at 300 degrees for 25 minutes. Serve with whipped cream or ice cream.

NS Tuna Steaks with Peperonata Sauce

NICK STELLINO

Serves 6

Here is an unusual pairing featuring a sauce that's reserved mostly for use with Italian sausages. The sauce is surprisingly good with tuna steaks. You should try it with chicken as well.

6 tuna steaks, each 6 ounces and about 1 inch thick
¼ teaspoon salt
¼ teaspoon pepper
1 teaspoon paprika
3 tablespoons Pompeian® Extra Light Olive Oil

FOR THE PEPERONATA SAUCE (yields 2½ cups):
3 tablespoons Pompeian® Extra Virgin Olive Oil
8 large garlic cloves, thickly sliced
½ teaspoon red pepper flakes (optional)
½ cup onion, finely diced
1 red bell pepper, cut into ½-inch dice
1 green bell pepper, cut into ½-inch dice
1 yellow bell pepper, cut into ½-inch dice
½ pound diced prosciutto or ham
Salt and pepper to taste
¾ cup Marsala wine, or port
1 tablespoon chopped fresh parsley, plus extra for garnish
1 tablespoon chopped fresh thyme
2 cups chicken stock
1 cup cream

TO PREPARE THE TUNA STEAKS:
Make the Peperonata Sauce (see below) and keep warm.

Sprinkle each tuna steak with salt, pepper and paprika; brush with some of the extra light olive oil. Cook on a grill over medium-high heat for 2 to 3 minutes per side. Alternatively, place the olive oil remaining after brushing the steaks in a sauté pan and heat over high heat until it starts sizzling. Then reduce the heat to medium and cook the tuna steaks in the oil, 2 minutes per side.

The above cooking times should give you a medium-rare center; if you like your tuna well done, continue cooking it a bit longer.

TO PREPARE THE PEPERONATA SAUCE:
In a large, deep sauté pan, heat the oil over medium-high heat, then add the garlic, red pepper flakes, onion and bell peppers. Sauté until soft, about 5 minutes. Increase the heat slightly. Add the prosciutto or ham, salt and pepper. Sauté about 2 to 3 minutes. Add the Marsala wine. Stir well and cook until the liquid is reduced by half. Stir in the parsley and thyme.

Add the chicken stock. Bring to a boil and then simmer for about 20 minutes.

Add the cream. Stir and continue to simmer for about another 10 to 15 minutes. The sauce is the proper consistency when it coats the back of a spoon.

TO SERVE:
Place the sauce on each serving plate. Top with a tuna steak and sprinkle with parsley. Serve immediately.

NS Pears in Red Wine Sauce
Pere al Vino Rosso

NICK STELLINO

Serves 4

4 large pears, peeled and cored
2 cups red wine
1 cup C&H® or Domino® sugar

Cut a small slice from the bottom of each of the pears so they will stand up straight in the saucepan without falling over. In a saucepan large enough to hold the pears, bring the wine and sugar to a boil over medium-high heat, stirring well. Once the mixture reaches a boil, cook for 3 more minutes.

Take the pan off the heat and gently place the pears, standing up, into the saucepan, being careful not to splash yourself with the hot wine-and-sugar mixture.

Place the pan back on the stove cook and the pears over medium-low heat—15 to 20 minutes for a firm texture or 30 to 40 minutes for a softer texture—basting the pears with the wine-and-sugar mixture every 5 minutes.

Turn off the heat and let the pears stand in the wine sauce until they reach room temperature. Use a slotted spoon to transfer each of the pears to a dessert dish, and top with plenty of the wine sauce.

CHEF'S NOTE: For an elegant presentation, serve the pears with sweet whipped cream or whipped mascarpone cheese, and top with toasted chopped pistachio nuts.

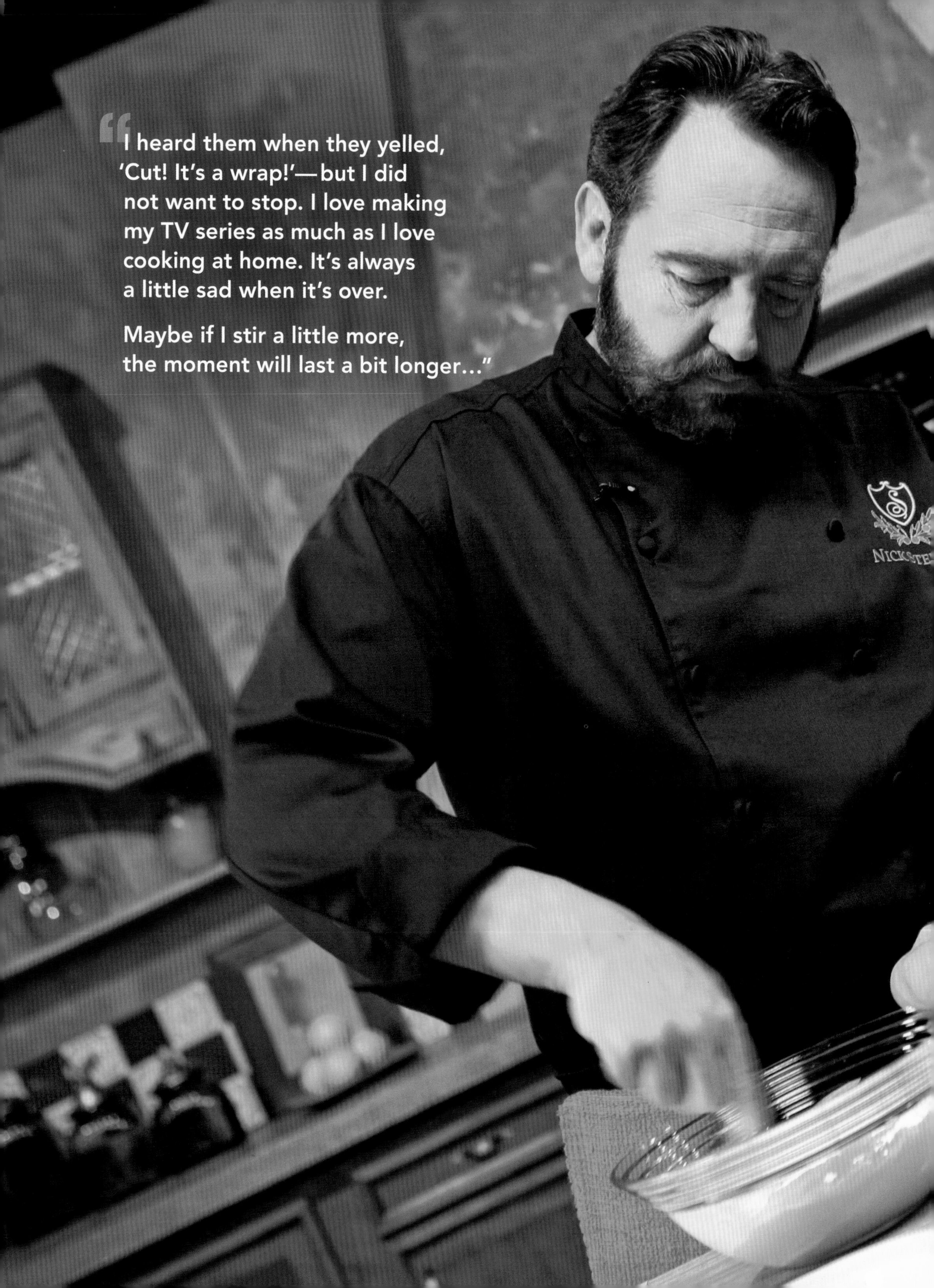

"I heard them when they yelled, 'Cut! It's a wrap!'—but I did not want to stop. I love making my TV series as much as I love cooking at home. It's always a little sad when it's over.

Maybe if I stir a little more, the moment will last a bit longer…"

GUEST CHEFS

CHEF DANNY BORTNICK Firefly | Washington, DC

Firefly's executive chef, Danny Bortnick, is no stranger to the DC Metro area. Born and raised in Maryland, Chef Bortnick is dedicated to supporting the region's bounty. His commitment to seasonal, sustainable and local food is evidenced by his ever-evolving menu, his relationships with local farmers, and his bountiful organic garden. The menu at Firefly features timeless dishes, updated with passion and whimsy, all designed to be approachable and delicious. Many menu items were inspired by meals from Danny's childhood. The simple, clean flavors and seasonal products shine on every plate. And he is glad to be leading the kitchen right in his own backyard.

firefly-dc.com

CHEF MICHAEL CIMARUSTI Providence | Los Angeles

Michael Cimarusti's passion and curiosity for food were ignited at an early age by his grandmother, Jo Cimarusti. In the great Italian culinary tradition, his grandmother, alongside his great-grandmother and aunts, made sure that every Sunday get-together was an event. Michael can trace his reverence for ingredients and proper technique back to those Sunday family meals.

providencela.com

CHEF NEAL FRASER Grace Restaurant | Los Angeles

Neal Fraser began his culinary career in Los Angeles at the age of 20, working as a line cook at Eureka Brewery and Restaurant, one of Wolfgang Puck's earliest restaurants. Inspired by this introduction to the life of a professional chef, Neal entered the Culinary Institute of America in 1990. As partner and executive chef at Grace, he serves his New American cuisine in an atmosphere perfectly designed to complement the ambitious flavors of one of Los Angeles' most revolutionary culinary talents.

gracerestaurant.com/index.php/grace/exec_neal

CHEF MICHAEL HILLYER The Capital Grille | Seattle

As executive chef of The Capital Grille, in Seattle, Michael Hillyer manages a kitchen staff of 25, and is responsible for all menu execution, culinary development and training. Michael draws inspiration from Pacific Northwest ingredients to create unique daily specials and seasonal menu features.

thecapitalgrille.com

CHEF LAURENT MANRIQUE AQUA | San Francisco

Chef Laurent Manrique has learned that combining simplicity with challenge involves walking a tightrope between passion for one's craft and a desire to constantly seek new opportunities. One of his most significant accomplishments in achieving that balance was the introduction of his renowned Gascon cooking at contemporary seafood-centric AQUA. "It was a whole new adventure," he says, "but one I was ready for. I needed to take on a challenge like this."

aqua-sf.com/aqua/chef

CHEF WALTER PISANO Tulio | Seattle

For Chef Walter Pisano, running an Italian restaurant was preordained. He is the son of a New York restaurateur, so the business runs in his blood; he is part of an East Coast Italian family, so the food is in his heart. Walter has been a longtime fixture on the Northwest restaurant scene, most notably for opening and operating Tulio Ristorante. Since its inception, Tulio has been a regular on the awards lists, receiving recognitions including *Seattle's Best Italian Restaurant*, *Best Business Lunch* and *Best Kept Secret*.

tulio.com/tulchef

CHEF KENT RATHBUN Abacus & Jasper's Restaurants | Texas

After rapidly rising through the ranks of some of the world's finest restaurants, Kent Rathbun created two of America's most talked-about restaurant concepts—Abacus and Jasper's, both winners of numerous awards. Kent's roots are firmly set in food. At the age of nine, he discovered his passion for culinary creativity and began learning the skills and techniques needed to become the renowned chef that he is today. In February 2008, Kent and his chef brother Kevin claimed victory over Bobby Flay on Food Network's *Iron Chef America*.

kentrathbun.com

CHEF HEATHER TERHUNE Atwood Café | Chicago

Executive Chef Heather Terhune has been messing up and cleaning up kitchens since she was a young girl, but it wasn't until college that she began her formal training. After attending the University of Missouri, where she received a Bachelor of Science degree in agriculture and hotel and restaurant management, Heather continued her education at the New England Culinary Institute, earning an associate's degree in culinary arts. She has worked for Kimpton Hotels & Restaurants since 1998.

atwoodcafe.com/atwchef

CHEF ELISE WIGGINS Panzano | Denver

From her beginnings in Louisiana to Texas, Colorado, Puerto Rico, Tennessee, and back to Colorado, Elise Wiggins has purposefully and progressively moved up through the ranks—honing kitchen skills and talents that have won numerous fine-dining awards and accolades. Panzano was named a *Top 5 Denver Restaurant* by the *Rocky Mountain News*, was included in *Zagat Survey's America's Top Restaurants* guide, and was given a four-star rating by *5280* magazine. Elise was named 2005's *Colorado Chef of the Year* by the American Culinary Federation.

panzano-denver.com

CHEF PATRICIA WILLIAMS District | New York

Patricia Williams has been the chef at District, adjacent to The Muse Hotel, since June 2006. Patricia is formerly of Morrell Wine Bar & Café and has worked as a chef in New York City for many years, at places such as Berkeley Bar and Grill and Butterfield 81.

districtnyc.com

"The director yelled, 'Action!,' and suddenly 40 hearts, including mine, started to beat as one. I have worked with the same crew of rascals for 14 years, and every time, it is a great experience. It is not about a TV show; it is about being part of a team that moves and thinks as a single unit. This is one of the great joys of my life! Without my team, there would be no TV show..."

thank you

Nothing worthwhile is ever achieved by a single individual; rather, it is the product of a team that works as a single unit.

I would like to take this opportunity to thank everyone on my whole team at KCTS/Seattle Public Television for all of their help. I am particularly thankful to Nicole Metcalf, my TV producer, and Dave Ko, my director, who helped me craft a beautiful television series featuring great food shots and visual storytelling.

My sincere thanks go to Lisa Moore, my book designer, and to the usual suspects, Jay Parikh, Tom Niemi and Don LaCombe, who have helped me enormously in my endeavors. Also, I would like to thank my culinary director, Bridget Charters, for keeping us on track and sane during the filming of our shows.

My wife, Nanci, was invaluable in helping me communicate my vision; without her, none of this would exist. The photographs in this book were shot by Therese Frare, and the book was edited with gentle charm by Pat Mallinson.

Lastly, I would like to thank all of my family and friends who have supported me in this odyssey.

What started as a little, impossible dream, handwritten on a yellow pad on the kitchen table of my small apartment some 25 years ago, has become a reality beyond my wildest dreams.

I am particularly grateful to these companies that have helped us make this book and the accompanying national television series a reality:

chsugar.com

dominosugar.com

davincipasta.com

pompeian.com

susanricetruffles.com

bdft.com

chefrevival.com

index

A
asparagus
Broiled Asparagus 30
Jasper's Tomato, Grilled Asparagus and Blue Cheese Salad with Grilled Chicken 84
Pasta with Ham, Mushrooms, Asparagus and Truffle Oil 18

B
beef
Grilled Fillet of, with Farro, Haricots Verts, Italian Sausage and Red Wine Sauce 33
Grilled Skirt Steak with Tomato-Infused Marinade 79
Meatballs with Tomato Sauce 15
Bourbon Creamed Corn 87
Broiled Asparagus 30
Bucatini with Pancetta and Ricotta 75
Butternut Squash with Parmesan, Roasted 31

C
Calamari Salad with Heirloom Tomatoes & Mint 24
Cauliflower Ragoût 55
Chestnut Soup and Nantucket Bay Scallops 57
chicken
Chicken Scaloppine with Leeks and Morels Sauce 41
Jasper's Tomato, Grilled Asparagus and Blue Cheese Salad with Grilled Chicken 84
Chipotle Barbecue Sauce 99
chocolate
Chocolate and Cherry Cake 112
Chocolate Espresso Cake with Raspberry Sauce 48
Easy Chocolate Mousse 95
Claufouti 126
Corn Relish 45
Crab and Lobster Burgers 45

D
Day Boat Halibut with Yukon Gold Potatoes and Chive Blossoms 23
desserts
Chocolate and Cherry Cake 112
Chocolate Espresso Cake with Raspberry Sauce 48
Claufouti 126
Dried Cherry-White Chocolate Bread Pudding 89
Easy Chocolate Mousse 95
Fried Palisade Peach Pie with Vanilla Gelato 105
Pears in Red Wine Sauce 132
Dried Cherry-White Chocolate Bread Pudding 89

E
Easy Chocolate Mousse 95

F
Fresh Chèvre and Panzanella Salad 69
Fried Palisade Peach Pie with Vanilla Gelato 105

G
goat cheese
Fresh Chèvre and Panzanella Salad 69
Grilled Salad with Goat Cheese 91
Palisade Peach Salad with Prosciutto-Crusted Goat Cheese Balls & Hazelnut-Mint Vinaigrette 107
Spinach Salad with Feta Cheese and Seedless Grapes 119
Green Eggs & Ham – Spinach, Ham and Cheese Quiche 16
Grilled Arctic Char with Chipotle Barbecue Sauce, Jicama Salad & Mango-Pineapple Salsa 99
Grilled Fillet of Beef with Farro, Haricots Verts, Italian Sausage and Red Wine Sauce 33
Grilled Salad with Goat Cheese 91
Grilled Skirt Steak with Tomato-Infused Marinade 79

H
ham
Green Eggs & Ham – Spinach, Ham and Cheese Quiche 16
Pasta with Ham, Mushrooms, Asparagus and Truffle Oil 18
Hamachi with Grapefruit-Basil Salad 59
Herb-Crusted Halibut with Fingerling Potatoes, Basil Nage, and Braised Romaine and Squash Blossoms 38
Herb Risotto with Heirloom Tomato Salad 68

J

Jasper's Tomato, Grilled Asparagus and Blue Cheese Salad with Grilled Chicken 84
Jicama Salad 99

L

Lobster Macaroni & Cheese with Truffle Oil 83

M

Mango-Pineapple Salsa 99
Maryland Crab Fritters with Herb Salad and Lemon Aïoli 97
Meatballs with Tomato Sauce 15
mushrooms
  Chicken Scaloppine with Leeks and Morels Sauce 41
  Mushroom Crêpes with Fonduta Sauce 110
  Pasta with Ham, Mushrooms, Asparagus and Truffle Oil 18
  Striped Bass with Pistachios and Wild Mushrooms 21

P

Palisade Peach Salad with Prosciutto-Crusted Goat Cheese Balls & Hazelnut-Mint Vinaigrette 107
pasta
  Bucatini with Pancetta and Ricotta 75
  Herb Risotto with Heirloom Tomato Salad 68
  Lobster Macaroni & Cheese with Truffle Oil 83
  Pasta with Cherry Tomatoes, Basil and Shrimp 50
  Pasta with Ham, Mushrooms, Asparagus and Truffle Oil 18
  Sautéed Day Boat Scallops with Truffle Risotto 36
peach
  Fried Palisade Peach Pie with Vanilla Gelato 105
  Palisade Peach Salad with Prosciutto-Crusted Goat Cheese Balls & Hazelnut-Mint Vinaigrette 107
  Wood-Grilled Pork Tenderloin with Peach Barbeque Sauce 86
pear
  Pears in Red Wine Sauce 132
  Watercress Salad with Poached Pears & Gorgonzola 121
pork
  Meatballs with Tomato Sauce 15
  Chops with Nancibella Sauce 115
  Wood-Grilled Pork Tenderloin with Peach Barbeque Sauce 86

Q

quiche
  Green Eggs & Ham – Spinach, Ham and Cheese Quiche 16

R

ricotta
  Bucatini with Pancetta and Ricotta 75
risotto
  Herb Risotto with Heirloom Tomato Salad 68
  Sautéed Day Boat Scallops with Truffle Risotto 36
Roasted Butternut Squash with Parmesan 31

S

salads
  Bitter Greens Salad 72
  Calamari Salad with Heirloom Tomatoes & Mint 24
  Fresh Chèvre and Panzanella Salad 69
  Grilled Salad with Goat Cheese 91
  Hamachi with Grapefruit-Basil Salad 59
  Jasper's Tomato, Grilled Asparagus and Blue Cheese Salad with Grilled Chicken 84
  Jicama Salad 99
  Palisade Peach Salad with Prosciutto-Crusted Goat Cheese Balls & Hazelnut-Mint Vinaigrette 107
  Spinach Salad with Feta Cheese and Seedless Grapes 119
  Tomato, Burrata and Arugula Salad 80
  Watercress Salad with Poached Pears & Gorgonzola 121
sauces
  Chipotle Barbecue 99
  Fonduta 110
  Grenobloise 55
  Leeks and Morels 41
  Nancibella 115
  Orange-Ginger 63
  Peach Barbeque 86
  Peperonata 128
  Raspberry 48
  Red Wine 33, 132
  Rosemary, Lemon and Honey 27
  Tartar 45
  Tomato 15
sausage, Italian
  Grilled Fillet of Beef with Farro, Haricots Verts, Italian Sausage and Red Wine Sauce 33
Sautéed Day Boat Scallops with Truffle Risotto 36
seafood
  Calamari Salad with Heirloom Tomatoes & Mint 24
  Chestnut Soup and Nantucket Bay Scallops 57
  Crab and Lobster Burgers 45
  Day Boat Halibut with Yukon Gold Potatoes and Chive Blossoms 23
  Grilled Arctic Char with Chipotle Barbecue Sauce, Jicama Salad & Mango-Pineapple Salsa 99
  Hamachi with Grapefruit-Basil Salad 59
  Herb-Crusted Halibut with Fingerling Potatoes, Basil Nage, and Braised Romaine and Squash Blossoms 38

Lobster Macaroni & Cheese with Truffle Oil 83
Maryland Crab Fritters with Herb Salad and Lemon Aïoli 97
Pasta with Cherry Tomatoes, Basil and Shrimp 50
Sautéed Day Boat Scallops with Truffle Risotto 36
Silky Corn Soup with Truffle Oil & King Crab Meat 76
Sole with Orange-Ginger Sauce 63
Striped Bass with Pistachios and Wild Mushrooms 21
Truffle-Salted Wild Salmon and Bitter Greens Salad 72
Tuna Steaks with Peperonata Sauce 128
Tuna Tartare with Grilled Toast 102
Venetian-Style Mussels 67
Wild King Salmon with Sauce Grenobloise and Cauliflower Ragoût 55

sides
Bourbon Creamed Corn 87
Broiled Asparagus 30
Chipotle Barbecue Sauce 99
Corn Relish 45
Jicama Salad 99
Mango-Pineapple Salsa 99
Roasted Butternut Squash with Parmesan 31
Tartar Sauce 45

Silky Corn Soup with Truffle Oil & King Crab Meat 76
Slow-Roasted Breast of Veal 125
Sole with Orange-Ginger Sauce 63

soup
Chestnut Soup and Nantucket Bay Scallops 57
Silky Corn Soup with Truffle Oil & King Crab Meat 76
Split Pea Chowder 123

spinach
Green Eggs & Ham – Spinach, Ham and Cheese Quiche 16
Spinach Salad with Feta Cheese and Seedless Grapes 119

Split Pea Chowder 123
Striped Bass with Pistachios and Wild Mushrooms 21

T

Tartar Sauce 45

tomato
Calamari Salad with Heirloom Tomatoes & Mint 24
Fresh Chèvre and Panzanella Salad 69
Herb Risotto with Heirloom Tomato Salad 68
Jasper's Tomato, Grilled Asparagus and Blue Cheese Salad with Grilled Chicken 84
Meatballs with Tomato Sauce 15
Pasta with Cherry Tomatoes, Basil and Shrimp 50
Tomato, Burrata and Arugula Salad 80
Tomato-Infused Marinade 79

Truffle-Salted Wild Salmon and Bitter Greens Salad 72
Tuna Steaks with Peperonata Sauce 128
Tuna Tartare with Grilled Toast 102

V

veal
Meatballs with Tomato Sauce 15
Slow-Roasted Breast of 125
Chops with Rosemary, Lemon and Honey Sauce 27

Venetian-Style Mussels 67

W

Watercress Salad with Poached Pears & Gorgonzola 121
Wild King Salmon with Sauce Grenobloise and Cauliflower Ragoût 55
Wood-Grilled Pork Tenderloin with Peach Barbeque Sauce 86

Turn your home
into your favorite restaurant!